THE RELATIONSHIT SHOW

S. COLE

Anika,
Grab some popcorn
and a whole bottle of
wine. You're in for a
treat!

D. Cole

The Relationshit Show

Editing: Laura Hull, Red Pen Princess

Cover Design: Book Cover Kingdom

Interior Formatting: Jess Bryant

❀ Created with Vellum

ALSO BY S. COLE

The Brookston Housewives Series

Sin in Suburbia

Secrets on Sapphire

Skeletons Amongst Sycamores

For every woman who is addicted to carrots and finds themselves eating carrots again and again even though they know they shouldn't eat the carrots because all carrots do is make your tummy hurt.
I feel your pain. We'll get through this.

The Relationshit Show

Hop aboard the hot mess express.
It's time to binge read your favorite show.

NOTE TO THE READER

Hello there. Let me introduce myself. My name is Cole. I'm a writer. I'm a writer with a bad case of writer's block, so I'm gonna try a thing here. I'm going to write in a way that's like I'm writing in my journal or bullshitting with a group of friends. That's what we are here, right? Friends?

I'm going to share everything that pops into my head regarding my past experiences and my present. My life. My story. My *lurv* story. Or lack thereof. I'm writing to you, friend. Yeah, you—the person whose eyes are scanning over these words, whose fingers will skim the pages as you continue through this book or will swipe on your device as you electronically turn the page or whose fingers are doing whatever it is your fingers do while you listen to my words through your speakers.

Well, here goes nothing . . .

PILOT EPISODE

One night, I was sitting on my floor. That reads like I don't do this a lot. Trust me, I do. My floor is very comfortable. Anyway, that particular night, however, I was drunk on wine—again, not a rarity—writing in my journal. Here, read it. Here's what I wrote that one night:

Dumped. Again. Seems to be the story of my life. Literally, my entire life. Twenty-seven years of being dumped time and time again. I should be numb to it by now, right? Aren't you? I mean, someone comes along and you feel all shiny and new and hopeful for what's to come. Then a warm hand touches you and looks inside and sees your potential and says yes, yes, this is the one. You're perfect for me. Yes. Then they take you home, fill you up, and when they're done, you're useless. You get thrown in the pile with all the other ones that came before you and it's on to the next one. Although, you may not know exactly what I'm talking about because you are just a journal. But on the other side of the same token, you should know exactly what I'm talking about because you're filled with my thoughts . . . my feelings . . . my heartaches and struggles and laughs and giggles and oh my Lord, I'm 27 fucking years old and I'm writing in my journal about boys—

scratch that—men. Nope. Scratch that again, I was right the first time—boys.

I need a soulmate, Journal. When I got my IUD put in at 25, I was told it was good for three years and then I could reinsert another one or, if I was ready to start a family by then, my doctor and I could discuss that instead. At 25, I was like "oh, that's perfect! 28? I'll definitely be starting a family by then. I'll be out of this town, living with my husband and y'all can take this shit out and he can shove his thing in and give me my baby." Yet, here I am. 27. And dumped. Again.

* * *

HEY THERE! You're back! Let's talk about The Phase. Oh, come on. We all know what phase I'm talking about. The Slut Phase, The Ho Phase, and my all-time favorite way to say it: The Slore Phase. We all go through it. Okay . . . well, most of us experience it and trust me, there is nothing to be ashamed of. This isn't a story meant to slut shame or bring up the double standard of how men can be as whore-ish as they want while women are supposed to keep their legs closed.

No, no, no.

This story is my story and how I am smack dab in the middle of my slore phase . . . yet again. Yes, you read that correctly. The Slore Phase, Part Deux. It happens, folks. I'm a twenty-seven-year-old living in a college town where I can't, for the life of me, snag a man for keeps. The men here, and I won't disclose where exactly, because that would just be plain rude. I'm sure you're trying to stalk my social media now to figure out where I might have lived while I wrote this story. If you find it, then oh well . . . I didn't tell you though, right? Let's be honest . . . I'm probably going to slip and tell you the name of the city eventually.

Anyway, I got sidetracked, didn't I? Before we continue,

let me share something with you about me—and you're about to get to know me oh so well—I have random thoughts that pop into my head and I do get easily sidetracked, so you might find my random thoughts scattered across some pages here and there. I've got to get them on paper, or they will bug the shit out of me. #lifeofawriter

And I got sidetracked about getting sidetracked. Let's start this sentence again.

The men here, in this college town, are too young. I'm staring down the tunnel to thirty and I am not getting any younger. Trust me. The demographic is pretty much summed up by boys (yes, I know I typed boys and not men) who are only concerned with booty and booze OR older, more seasoned men, who are happily married with children of their own. Oh! And can't forget the grandkids.

So, you see. Snagging a man. Here. Is just about damn near impossible. At least for keeps. For fun? Now that's a whole other story. But don't fret, I'm sharing all the stories within these pages. I hope you're in for a wild ride. Hop aboard the hot mess express and get ready for some treats.

Now, the question is, where should I begin? Well, I'm sure you're wondering why I'm struggling to breathe, bawling on the floor, trying not to spill this bottle of wine? Right? (I told you, I drink wine on my floor quite a bit). Let's just start from right now and we'll see where my brain decides to take us . . . sits and ponders . . . sits and ponders . . . no, no, that's not a good place. Let's start from the beginning, where it all started. Where the love began . . .

I was sitting under one of the playground fixtures all alone. Eight years old and with an imagination running wild as ever while I hid. I was new to the school and hadn't made any friends yet. You see, my dad was in the military and this was my third school in the short three years of starting my education.

There's no telling what I was thinking up when it hit me. And by *it*, I mean a ball. A basketball came flying from nowhere and smacked me right in the face. I was in such shock, I couldn't even cry. That shit hurt like a bitch. With my mouth open and my hand on my cheek, I heard something else coming for me and it was coming fast. I quickly looked around and then the swift movement stopped.

"Are you okay?" A tall, gangly, black kid with big brown eyes covered with glasses looked down at me.

When I didn't answer, he kind of just rocked back and forth on his feet and pursed his lips.

"Uhm . . .," he started.

"Yeah, I'm fine." I rolled the ball back to him and turned away, clutching my hand back to my cheek.

"Sorry," he mumbled as he walked away.

A tear rolled down my burning cheek. I turned back around and watched him running back to the basketball court.

It was the first time I realized I had a crush on a boy. It was the first time a boy made me cry. Sure, the tears were from being accidentally hit with the basketball and didn't necessarily hurt my feelings, but it wouldn't be the last time a boy caused tears to fall. It wouldn't be the last time *he* caused them.

But I've dug too far back, let's jump six years and go from there. Fourteen. The year I got my first real boyfriend. My first year of high school. The start to the best and worst times of my life.

EPISODE 1

THE PUP

I'll start off this episode by telling you why this man is called The Pup. I feel like I must explain, because I am in no way calling him a dog. I mean, in some situations throughout our relationship, he was kind of a dog . . . but I was also a bitch at times while we were together. However, in this instance, he's simply being called The Pup because we had that thing called puppy love.

We started dating, if that's what you can even call it at that age, at a mere fourteen years old. Granted, the relationship lasted for five years, but we were just babies. So yeah, he's The Pup. He was my first experience of love and my first heartache. We've somewhat kept up over the years and I'd like to say we're kind of friends. So, if you happen to be reading this, Pup, I wish you the best.

I was a freshman in high school and there was this one guy I was kind of talking to. I'll call him Rob. Rob was one of those popular kids. He played football, he was the class clown, and he was always getting in trouble. We were in drama together and he cracked me up. Rob and I also had

English together and our seats just happened to be next to each other.

Across the room was Pup. I thought he was cute, but I didn't pay too much attention to him at first because of Rob. However, I always felt his eyes on me, and we would shyly smile at each other occasionally. Well, there were a couple of days Rob was suspended. With him gone, Pup took his shot. He partnered up with me on an in-class project. I really noticed how cute he was, and he smelled so good—like baby lotion and spices.

I talked to my friends about Pup and how I didn't know what to do because I liked Rob too. One of my friends told me I would be dumb not to take a chance with Pup. Rob was just a playboy and it would never work out. *Like we were searching for our soulmates as freshmen in high school.*

* * *

ONE DAY I was at school early for a Beta Club meeting. Yes, I was in Beta Club (it was kind of the nerdy club, but it looked good on that college resume) and yes, this story will loop back around. Trust me.

I thought we were supposed to meet up in front of the Freshman Building, but when I got there, no else from the club was there. I pulled out my phone to call one of my friends and that's when an administrator just showed up out of nowhere. Out of thin air. To this day, I still have no clue where the hell she came from.

"Excuse me, but what do you think you're doing with your phone out, young lady?"

"I'm trying to call my friend to see where the Beta Club is meeting." I hung up the phone and looked at the woman, confused.

"You know there is a *no cell phone* policy."

I was stumped. "I'm sorry. I thought that was only during school hours. And since class hasn't started yet, I thought it'd be okay."

"The rule applies to the property, not the hours. You can't have your phone out at all while you're on school property."

Now, that didn't seem right. You mean to tell me I can't have my phone out during a football game or after school when I'm on school property to call my parents? I thought all of that, but when I was in high school, I was a really good kid and I would never have even thought about talking back to an authority figure. Not unless I wanted to get an ass whooping when I got home.

"I'm sorry, ma'am. I didn't know."

"Okay. Well, I'm still going to have to take your phone from you. You can pick it up in the Freshman Building office tomorrow morning."

I nodded my head and followed the woman into the front office. When we walked into the building, I saw that friend I was trying to call. After signing my phone over, I walked out and joined the group.

"What happened, Cole?"

"I was trying to call you to see where everyone was, but apparently we're not supposed to be on our phones before class either."

"Oh damn. That sucks. Yeah, we met inside."

I stared at my friend with an irritated grin on my face. "Yeah. I see that now."

That night, I got sick. Like *vomiting all over the place* sick. I couldn't go to school the next day, and after explaining to my dad why I had gotten my phone taken away, he agreed to go pick it up for me on his way home from work.

When he got home, he handed my phone over.

"The woman said you were very polite."

I told you I was a good kid.

"She said it was very clear that you just didn't understand the policy. So, I guess not having your phone for two days was punishment enough."

"Thanks, Dad!"

I turned my phone back on and saw I had a voicemail. I went up to my room to listen to it.

"Hey, Cole," a deep voice came through the phone—well, deep for an adolescent male. "It's Pup. I didn't see you at school today. I hope everything is okay. So, anyway, I was wondering if you wanted to be my girlfriend?"

With wide eyes, I looked at my phone like it was going to say 'Ha! Just joking.' I pressed play again.

"Hey, Cole, it's Pup. I didn't see you at school today. I hope everything is okay. So, anyway, I was wondering if you wanted to be my girlfriend?"

I exited out of the voicemails and looked to my call log. There was no phone number for a missed call. That's when I realized since my phone was off, sitting in the drawer in the front office of the Freshman Building the night before, it had gone straight to voicemail. No number to save.

How could I call Pup back to let him know 'Yes! Yes! I would love to be your girlfriend'? He probably thought I was ignoring him. It had been a whole day. If I was ignoring him, then I didn't want to be his girlfriend—that's probably what he's thinking—but I do want to be his girlfriend. 'I do want to be your girlfriend. I DO!'

Right before I ran down the stairs to ask my mom what to do, the phone started ringing. I didn't recognize the number on the screen. Could it be?

"Hello?"

"Hey. Cole?"

"This is she."

"Hey, it's Pup."

"Hey! What's up?"

"How's it going? You weren't in class today. Is everything okay?"

"It's better than it was. I've been sick."

"Oh no. How are you feeling?"

"Not too bad. I think whatever it was is passing. I'd been vomiting non-stop, but I went to the doctor today and they gave me a suppository and stuck a needle in my butt."

Silence. I nervously laughed as I just realized that even though I had gotten a shot in my ass, I was still vomiting. Obviously, the medicine didn't help word vomit.

Pup laughed. His laugh was genuine and sweet, and I think that's when I started to fall in love.

"Yeah . . . so, anyway . . ." I couldn't think of anything else to say.

"Did you happen to get my voicemail from last night?" he asked nervously.

"I did. I just listened to it actually, right before you called. Sorry I didn't call you back. I got my phone taken away at school before I got sick and my dad just gave it back to me and since it was off, the phone didn't save your number, so I didn't have a way to call you back. Sorry."

Seriously? Do they make butt shots that cure word vomit?

"It's okay. So, you listened to it then?"

"Yes."

One word. I can handle one-word answers.

"Well . . . what do you think?"

"Yes."

"You'll be my girlfriend?"

"Yes, I'll be your girlfriend."

Whatever happened to it being that easy anyway? Dating used to be so simple . . .

* * *

AFTER THAT, it didn't take long for us to form the typical high school relationship. We interlaced our fingers as we walked through campus. We snuck kisses in between classes. We gave each other notes as we passed in the hall. Almost every weekend we were at each other's houses. My parents loved him and his parents loved me. It was great and too boring to continue talking about in this book.

Freshman year came and went. Our sophomore year, Pup transferred to a different high school. The schools were close, but it wasn't the same as being at the same school. I didn't get to see him every day, but we continued to hang out most weekends. He was one of the starters on his school's football team, so I would go watch him play most Friday nights. A friend once told me I was like the perfect trophy wife. I'm still not sure if that was a compliment or an insult.

Sophomore year and junior year were much of the same and, again, too boring to write about. Sorry, Pup. If you're reading this, I really did enjoy the beginning of our relationship, but that's just not what this book is about.

There was a girl I suspected was into Pup and he said they were just friends. The girl and I went to lunch one weekend, and I actually really liked her. We became pretty good friends after that, so I set aside my initial concerns. Hopefully my initial thoughts were wrong, and I wasn't just stupid.

I'll throw in a funny thing from those early years that I'll never forget. It was junior prom. The group I was with decided to go bowling after the dance. We got our shoes and our names set up in the computer. Everyone was laughing and having a good time. It was Pup's turn. He picked up the ball and stuck his fingers in the appropriate holes. He lifted it up to his face and stared down the lane like he knew what he was doing. Pup brought the ball behind his back, he swooshed it forward, and then he let the ball go . . . all the way across four lanes. I'm not exaggerating here. The ball literally flew across the four lanes to our left before coming down with a thud.

It was the best part of the whole night. That being said, we obviously didn't have sex.

Actually, up to that point, we hadn't at all. We were pretty good kids. It wasn't until we were freshmen in college that we lost our virginity to each other. It's really kind of sweet when you think about it. But, again, sweet is not the overarching theme of this story.

* * *

COLLEGE . . . it was the best of times, it was the worst of times. That's where things kind of got real sticky between us —literally and figuratively.

Pup and I broke up briefly while I tried to sort out my feelings for my best friend, The Zombie. Don't fret, I'll get into that later. He gets his own long ass episode. Pup and I eventually got back together. It was early in our freshman year; I want to say September or October.

Just like high school, we went to different schools. I attended school in Georgia, and he went to a small private college in South Carolina on a football scholarship. When we first got back together, I drove to see him and that's where the deed was done, and we were no longer innocent little puppies. We were grown ass dogs now.

One night, I was staying with Pup at his apartment on campus. The fire alarm went off and when we both woke up and realized what was happening, we started freaking out. Not because we thought there was an actual fire, but because I wasn't supposed to be in Pup's room. Since it was a private university, they had their own set of rules and they could say things like 'no opposite sex sleepovers allowed'.

We got out of bed, raced to get our clothes on, and then stared at each other for a few beats.

"Get in the closet?"

"What?"

"Just hide in the closet, Cole."

"What if there's a real fire?"

"There's not a real fire. They talked about doing a drill soon in our last building meeting."

The alarm was blaring now.

"I've got to get outside before they start the count. Just get in the closet. Please."

What could I do? I sighed heavily and shut my ass in the closet, hoping and praying I wasn't going to die burning alive in there.

A few moments later, the alarm stopped. I never heard the front door to the apartment open or any voices entering the room. All of a sudden, the doorknob on the closet started moving.

Fuck. What if they were doing room checks? Now that I think about it, I'm not sure why I was so worried. I didn't go to school there. What could they have done to me?

My heart was beating fast as the doorknob continued to turn. What was I going to say? What would happen to Pup if they found me in here? The door popped open, and just as I was about to come up with the best excuse ever, I saw the biggest smile. It was Pup.

"Well, that was quick."

He kissed me on my forehead, and we went back to bed.

* * *

ONE WEEKEND, I was going up to see Pup when he was going to have a late football practice. He told me he would leave the key for me under the mat, and I could just hang out in his room until he got there. I'm not sure when it happened, but at some point, while I laid on his bed, I must have gotten really comfortable. I fell asleep.

I was *real* comfortable lying there. Drool was falling from my mouth onto the mattress. Suddenly, I was awakened from my sleep by banging and all kinds of loud noises going on. My first thought was to hop up and hide in the closet again before one of the building assistants found me in the room.

When I finally got the nerve to open my eyelids, I saw rustling behind the blinds on the window. The blinds started moving inward, and I saw a big leg push its way inside. The blinds lifted, and I was just about to have a heart attack when I recognized who the big leg belonged to. We made eye contact as Pup straddled the windowsill.

"What are you doing?" he asked me, exasperated.

I laughed. "What are *you* doing?

"I'm trying to get in my house. I've been out here for almost half an hour. What have you been doing?"

"I'm sorry, babe. I fell asleep."

"How did you think I was going to get in? You have my key!"

"Where are your roommates?"

They were also on the football team.

"They went to get food." He shook his head.

"So . . . are you going to come in or nah?"

* * *

MOST OF MY and Pup's time together was great. I'd say we were good for about 90% of it. The older we got, the further apart we grew. We were at different schools in different states, and the distance was wearing on us. On top of that, we were growing up. We had met when we were just fourteen

17

years old. Fast forward five years to us at nineteen, and we were just discovering who we were.

By the time our break-up became official, I was interested in another guy. I remember I used to hope Pup would cheat on me, so I could get out of the relationship. I wanted him to cheat on me, so I didn't have to feel bad about my growing feelings for another guy. They say be careful what you wish for.

Pup did end up cheating on me. Ultimately, it's not what ended our relationship, because I didn't find out that he had strayed until after we had decided to let each other go. Some nights I suspected it was happening, but I never got confirmation while we were still together.

When we broke up, I told Pup I was starting to like someone else and we had hung out a few times. It was in groups, but still, I liked him, and he was over at my house. Things between Pup and I were pretty sour, and we were trying our darndest to stop talking to each other, but it was hard. He was a huge part of my life and essentially my best friend for five years. I wasn't used to not talking to him every day.

We were doing pretty well with the whole not communicating thing when one night I got a strange message on Facebook. Some girl had sent me a novel-length message telling me about her relationship with Pup and how he used to talk to her about me and how they had started hooking up around my birthday. Mind you, my birthday was six months prior to the end of our relationship. Also, why the fuck did this bitch know when my birthday was?

I called Pup the next morning and told him about the message. He then proceeded to tell me that most of what she had said was true and he was sorry. I asked him why she felt the need to message me in the first place, and he told me she was mad at him. She had been out and drunk and had wanted Pup to pick her up. When he refused, she told him she was going to message me. He didn't believe she really would, and he didn't pick her up. And so, there we were.

I asked him to please not have his hos messaging me. I had nothing to do with his love life anymore and I didn't need to be involved any further. He apologized again and that was that. For a while anyway.

A few months passed and life without Pup was going fine and dandy. I was getting used to the fact that he was no longer my best friend and things were looking up. The tears had dried and the anger had subsided. Then one of his roommates texted me and said he was graduating and asked if I wanted to come to his graduation. Pup's roommates and I had gotten close over the years. They cracked me up and were good people. I told him I would definitely be there.

I asked my roommate, Andrea, to go with me. She said she would, and we made a road trip of it. We got there, found a place to park, and got a seat inside the building where the graduation was being held.

The graduation was like all graduations. Long and boring and exciting all at once. I knew a good handful of the graduates, and I clapped and screamed when their names were called. I didn't see Pup during the ceremony and that was okay with me. I made sure I looked really good though just in case I ran into him.

After the ceremony, I met up with the guys who had invited me to give them hugs and well wishes. We took pictures together and talked for a bit before Andrea and I headed back to my car to leave.

While we were taking the photos, there was a girl who was kind of hovering around the group the entire time I was there. I finally locked my eyes on Pup while I was talking to the graduates and not soon after, this girl, I'll call her

Chevron thanks to her black and white chevron-patterned dress, started talking to Pup with her friend.

Afterward, when Andrea and I made it back to the car, I asked her if she thought that girl was into Pup.

"It looked like they were just friends," she said.

I drove us all the way back home without another thought on Chevron.

A few days later, I posted the pictures from the graduation on Facebook. The guys had done the same and tagged me in the few I was in. I was looking at the photos and noticed a comment from Chevron on the one that just had me in it. She posted three laughing emojis and that was it.

W

T

F

I didn't know that girl. At all. And now she was laughing at me. For what? I hadn't a clue. It didn't take long for me to find out that there was a thing between Pup and Chevron. She lived in the apartment below him, and apparently, they were "best friends." I still couldn't tell you why she laughed on my picture, but during the months to come, all the anger I had for Pup reared its ugly head. I thought I had gotten rid of it, but obviously it had been sewn up with my broken heart and just needed to be poured out for good.

Chevron and Pup dated for a good long while and eventually I got over it. About a year or two after we'd graduated from college, and long after any hate for one another had dissipated, Pup and I decided to get drinks to celebrate his birthday. I asked him how things were going with him and Chevron and that's when he told me they broke up. For a split second, I wanted to send her three laughing emojis.

EPISODE 2

✼

THE UP AND DOWN

*M*y stomach was unsettled, and my hands were shaky. It was the first day of a new beginning. College. I was just a number on a huge college campus. And when I say huge, I mean *huge*. Like over 30,000 students huge. And then there was me. Small, petite, caramel skinned, with straightened hair pulled back into a ponytail. This was all before the natural hair look came into style.

The yellow and black Vera Bradley backpack I needed so desperately was snug on my back and I had my notebook pressed firm against my chest. I was alone and waiting for the doors to open to my first ever lecture hall class. I had been to a couple of my other classes already, but they were all average sized. This one, however, had hundreds of students in it.

Do I look natural standing here? Weird? Awkward? What do I do with my hands?!

I pulled out my cell phone from the side pocket of my backpack and started toying with it. I didn't have any text messages or missed calls. My fingers fumbled over the keys as I tried to make it look like I was doing something.

Anything. I put my phone back in the pocket and clutched the notebook back to my chest.

Someone was staring at me. I could feel it. I nervously—and probably awkwardly—glanced around as I tried to be nonchalant and catch the eyes watching me because believe me, someone was burning a hole into my face. I had almost given up looking when I caught him. Two of the most amazing eyes I had ever stared into were on me. They were big, brown, beautiful eyes. Never before had I seen eyes as large and as bright as his. They fit though, matching the gorgeous grin splayed across his face.

After being locked into each other for what felt like forever, I coyly smiled and turned back around, almost tripping over my own two feet. I heard him laugh, but I didn't dare turn back to face him.

"You're gonna marry him." The voice was as clear as day; however, no one had truly said the words. *Going crazy now, huh?* They say it's the late teens and early twenties when people start to lose it.

I didn't know why the thought had crossed my mind, but it was something I naively believed for the years to come.

I was in a relationship with Pup when I first saw him. I can't think of a crazy, unique nickname to sum up this guy or what we had, so I'll simply call him B. My friends or anybody else who was even slightly involved in this situation and knows who I am, will know who B is. They all know most of what went on in this relationshit, so I'm not too worried about keeping his identity that secret. However, B is all you're going to get from me because it is from the rest of the world (as if the entire world is going to read this book) that I will protect his identity and reputation because I am somewhat of a nice person . . . and I don't want to get sued.

Like I said, I was in a relationship with Pup that first day B and I locked eyes. I thought he was attractive, and that strange thought of marriage crossed my mind, but that was all there was the rest of that semester. We had Biology 1101 together, and we were two in a class of 300. I saw him walk into class most days and I would stare at him briefly and only got slightly jealous when I saw him flirting with the girl he sat next to.

After that first semester of college, I didn't see B again freshman year. It wasn't until the second semester of my second year in college that I saw those big brown eyes again. That was when things weren't going that great with Pup, as you read in the previous episode.

There was an event in the student plaza area on campus. I think it was a barbeque or something similar that one of the black fraternities was hosting. I was with my two room-mates, Andrea and Cici, and some of Cici's dance team team-mates. We were standing around, swaying to the music, when the music stopped and whistles started blowing and one of the fraternities began doing their stroll. They were in their line, dancing and moving their bodies in sync to a rhythm their brothers had been doing for years. I looked over and that's when it happened again. We locked eyes. B was leading the group and the way his body moved to the beat had me really turned on. I asked Cici's teammates if they knew who he was, and they told me his name. B and I smiled at each other and again parted ways without saying a word.

A few weeks later, Cici, Andrea, and I were in a study room in the Learning Center on campus. We all had tests coming up and were trying to cram in some last-minute study sessions. I was on Facebook taking a quick break when I decided to type in B's name. He popped up immediately and I sent him a friend request. I had just gotten back to studying when a notification dinged on my laptop. I went back to Facebook and saw B had accepted my friend request. I squealed with excitement.

"What is it?" Andrea asked.

"He accepted my friend request!"

Andrea and Cici already knew who I was talking about. I had been talking about him for weeks at this point, not knowing if it would be a good idea to engage with him or not. There was still Pup after all.

"Did he now?" Cici closed her notebook.

"Yes. I don't know what to do. Should I message him?"

"Uh . . . yeah." Cici looked at me with an expression of *duh.*

"What about Pup?" Andrea asked.

Andrea had gone to high school with me and she knew Pup.

"A simple message wouldn't hurt," Cici chimed in.

I looked from Andrea to Cici and bit my bottom lip. "Right? I'm just gonna say hello."

They both just smiled at me and waited for me to type out the message.

Me: *Hey you*

I pressed send and the three of us started studying again.

"Y'all want to order some pizza?" Andrea asked.

"Oh, yeah! I'm starving," Cici interjected.

"I'll look up some pizza places that will deliver here."

I minimized my notes and that's when I noticed I had a message on Facebook waiting for me.

B: *Hey there*

"What is it?" Andrea asked. She must have seen my eyes widen.

"He messaged me back."

"What did he say?" Cici asked.

"He just said 'hey there'."

"Well, what are you going to say in response?"

"I don't know . . ."

Me: So, I think we had Bio together last year.

Smooth move.

B: Lol, yeah. I think you're right. So, how have you been?

That's how it all began. A simple 'hey you' kickstarted years on the most brutal emotional roller coaster I had ever willingly strapped myself into. As you know, Pup and I eventually broke up. Things with B heated up so quickly, I should have known I was going to get burned.

* * *

ONE NIGHT, a few weeks after B and I had started talking, Andrea, Cici, and I, along with some of our other friends, went to a foam party. It was wet and wild and ruined a pair of my favorite shoes. While we were there, I ran into B. I asked him if he wanted to come over after the party. He said he was going to be tired, so he wasn't sure if he would make it.

"You can spend the night," I said as I looked up at him, my arms wrapped around his waist.

He smiled. "You sure?"

"Yeah," I said as I thought about it very briefly. Like a millisecond, if that.

"Okay. I'll text you after." He quickly pecked my forehead and wiggled out of my grasp.

When the party was over, Andrea, Cici, and I picked up

food from McDonald's and headed home. We all changed out of our wet clothes and ate our food in the living room.

"So, is B coming over?" Andrea asked.

"He said he was," I answered with my mouth full of room temperature fries.

My phone beeped and a text from B told me he was on his way over.

Not long after, Andrea and Cici had retreated to their rooms. I was waiting in the living room when I heard a light knock on the door. I looked out of the peephole and saw B standing in the breezeway.

I answered the door and we smiled at each other, both with hooded eyelids. Lust and lethargy.

"Hey," he said as he walked past me into the living room.

"Hey."

He plopped down on the couch. I walked into the living room and stood next to him. I reached my hand out for him to take. He grabbed my hand and I looked at him.

"Come on." I urged him off the couch with a tug of his hand and guided him into my bedroom.

I won't go into too much detail here, but I'm sure you know what happened next. The two of us ended up in my bed with B on top of me. We kissed and one thing led to another. A condom was ripped open. He slid the rubber on and he entered me once. I moaned. Twice. I tried to catch my escaping breath.

The end.

Seriously. That was it.

"I'm sorry," he said as he rolled off me.

"I haven't had sex in so long," he stuttered. "I'm sorry."

I grimaced slightly. "It's okay." I mean, what else was I supposed to say? "We can always try again." I touched his shoulder.

"I didn't bring anymore condoms."

"Well . . . okay. That's okay."

"I'm really sorry. I didn't know . . ." his voice trailed off.

"Really"—I looked him in the eye the best I could with the lights off—"it's okay." I smiled genuinely and got up to go to the restroom.

That was the first time B and I had sex. I should have just let that be it, but I went back for more.

* * *

B and I dated for years, and over that time, the two of us attended lots and lots of parties. However, we never attended the parties *together*. He was a member of one of the black fraternities on campus and he was one of the more "popular" guys in the group. He could dance and sing and had a great personality and it seemed that everyone loved B.

We were at some party his frat was hosting. It was being held downtown and of course my girls and I were there. Cici and I had done some major pregaming and were definitely drunk before we got there. Andrea wasn't a fan of alcohol, so she was our designated driver and was sober as sober can be.

The party was fun. We danced with random guys, belted out songs without a care in the world, and as was always the case, eventually took our heels off. I saw B a number of times throughout the party. We danced once and talked briefly, but he spent most of his time with his frat brothers or with his crotch up against other women's asses. I was jealous whenever I saw it happen at parties, but I never said anything to him. It was just dancing, right?

I'm not sure exactly what happened. I couldn't tell you why we were arguing, but we were. And it was bad. B was walking through the crowd with me hanging onto him. My fingers were wrapped in his shirt and I was bawling my eyes out as he drug me, barefooted, through the crowd. He wasn't dragging me on purpose. He was trying to get away and I wouldn't let go. Eventually, we made it outside. There was less of a crowd and B was able to break free of my grasp. He grabbed onto my wrist when I tried to grab him again.

"B, please," I cried.

"Cole, let go. Seriously, let go of me." He looked at me with hurt and anger clouding those beautiful brown eyes.

"Don't go," I sobbed, "please."

People were starting to look at us.

"I'm leaving. I've gotta get outta here," he said sternly.

"No. Don't go."

He dropped my wrist and pushed it toward me. He turned to leave and I grabbed onto his shirt again. He turned again quickly and faced me.

"Cole." He stared me in the eyes. "I am leaving. You need to stay here with your friends. Do not follow me."

I let go of his shirt and he left. I stood alone outside, watching him go. I heard laughter behind me and turned to see a group of girls looking at me with huge grins as they whispered to one another. I sat down on a nearby bench and sobbed into my hands. When I looked down, I realized my shirt was twisted and my sticky bra was coming out of the top of my shirt. I had just fixed it with tear-soaked fingers when I felt an arm wrap around my shoulder.

"Cole . . ."

I looked up. It was one of B's brothers.

"B said you were out here. Come on. I'm gonna take you to your friends."

He gave me his hand and I followed him back inside, crying as we went. We made it back to Andrea and Cici. He asked me if I was okay and I just nodded. He left and Andrea and Cici took me home.

You would think this would have been the end, but it wasn't. Unfortunately, there's more.

* * *

IT WASN'T ALL BAD. There were definitely good times. Why else would I stick around so long? There was one Valentine's Day B had surprised me.

He graduated a semester before I did and moved back in with his parents. It was a little less than an hour away, but still far enough away it wasn't worth the drive in the middle of the week. Valentine's Day was during the week that year.

One of my best friends, Katie, and I decided we were going to be each other's Valentine and go out for dinner together. She came over to my apartment and we drank some wine while I finished getting ready and then out the door we went.

As we walked down the front steps, I noticed a car parked near mine with its headlights on. When we got closer to my car, I realized I recognized the car. It was B's. I smiled when I saw him get out, and he looked at me slightly confused.

"Where are you going?" he asked as he looked over at Katie.

She smiled and waved and got into the car.

"Me and Katie are going to dinner. We don't have dates tonight, so we were just gonna go with each other. What are you doing here?"

"I was coming to surprise you for Valentine's Day. I figured we could go see a movie or something." He reached out to give me a hug.

I grabbed his hands and leaned in, accepting his embrace.

"Well, I can see—"

He interrupted, saying "No, no. Go hang out with your friend. You didn't know I was coming. I can go chill with some of the bruhs until you get back."

"You don't mind? You drove all this way."

"I don't mind. Go have fun."

We kissed each other quickly and went our separate ways. After a great dinner date with Katie, B came back and we had a good Valentine's Day date of our own.

* * *

B CAME BACK THAT TIME, but there was another not-so-great time when he did just the opposite.

It was my 21st birthday. My childhood best friend, Biff, came into town to visit. My birthday is in June, so it was over summer break. A lot of my friends didn't stay in town over the summer, but I was paying for an apartment, so I might as well stay, right? That being said, Andrea and Cici were gone and couldn't make it back for drinking festivities that weekend. Our old roommate who had graduated already, Sissy, was going to come back to go out with me and Biff and a few of my other friends who were still in town. B said he would just come to the apartment after and spend the night, so I could enjoy a night out with my girls. He also wasn't really into drinking, so he knew he wouldn't have fun. And by not really into drinking, I mean he didn't drink at all.

Biff got there early and we hung out around the house, dancing to the music we grew up with and drinking cheap wine. She baked me cupcakes while I napped and we went shopping before it got dark. Nightfall hit and out we went. Sissy and my other friends met us at the bars. I had on a sash and blue suede heels. I got lots of free shots and took tons of pictures with strangers. I still have most of those pictures somewhere on my phone.

After partying for a few hours, Biff and I headed back to my apartment and I sobered up slightly waiting for B to get there. Biff and I had set up an air mattress in the living room for her and we were lying on it when someone knocked on the door. It was B.

When he came in, I introduced him to Biff and the two of us headed into my room. After I shut the door behind us, he gave me my present—a nice bottle of sparkling moscato. We talked for a bit. He asked me how my night was. I showed him pictures and then we started kissing. We both got into our birthday suits and he gave me the second half of my present.

We fell asleep, and an hour or two after we shut our eyes, B woke me up.

"I've got to go," he whispered.

I rubbed my eyes and stared at the clock.

"It's 5:30 in the morning. Why?" I croaked.

"One of my frat brothers has a flat tire. He's stuck on the side of the road and I need to go help him." He started climbing out of the bed, looking for his clothes.

"Isn't there someone else who can help him? It's my birthday, B."

He zipped up his pants and grabbed his backpack. "I'll come back."

"What?" I asked.

"I'll come back. Just let me go help him change the tire and I'll come back. I promise. It should only take a couple of hours, if that."

"You promise?"

"Yeah, Cole. I'll be back, okay?"

"Okay . . ." I pouted. "Just lock the door on your way out. Call me when you're on the way back. I'll put my phone on loud."

"Okay," he said softly, leaning into the bed to kiss my forehead.

I woke up close to 9 and realized I was still alone. I picked up my phone and there were no missed calls. No texts. I called B's phone and he didn't answer. I waited another thirty minutes and tried again. No answer. I text

S. COLE

him and waited for another half an hour. There was no response. I put my phone down and curled into a ball and started crying.

Through my quiet sobs, I heard a rap on my bedroom door. I didn't say anything but continued crying. Biff walked in the room.

"What's wrong?" she asked.

"He left me on my birthday."

I started crying harder and Biff climbed up onto the bed and crawled under the covers next to me.

"I'm naked," I said loudly through streams of tears.

We both were quiet for a second, then Biff just wrapped her arms around my shoulder and we both started cracking up.

* * *

Like I've mentioned before, it wasn't all bad.

Yet again, there was a party. His fraternity hosted it and it is still one of the biggest parties of the year. It's the event his frat was known for and one a lot of people looked forward to.

It was my junior year and my friends and I couldn't wait for this particular party. I even had some friends coming into town to attend the party with us. The interesting thing is, those friends were actually Pup's teammates. We all got along pretty well and they knew I went to the school hosting the party and they wanted to be there. They hit me up and I told them they could stay with me. It was only slightly awkward. I tried to invite Pup, to be nice and all, but he was dating Chevron, so he declined.

Anyway . . . the guys showed up the day of the party. They brought liquor, which, when added to what was already in the apartment, was plenty to get us all pretty wasted. Day drinking is very bad. I wish I would have listened to that line in J-Kwon's song "Tipsy" a little more closely.

Somehow, we all managed to get dressed. Andrea, Cici, some of our other girlfriends, and I all managed to apply our makeup without looking like hot messes and slide our feet into stilettos. (This was before I discovered I could get just as many free drinks in a pair of flats.) All of us got into two separate cars and off we went.

We blasted music in the car I was in, and I had my Smirnoff Ice in my hand as I hung out the window. I sang along to the song and cracked up with my girls in the back seat. We didn't make it far when all of a sudden, my Smirnoff Ice was no longer in the bottle. It was somehow all over me. I was soaked.

"The fuck?" I said.

"Uh oh," Andrea said from the front seat.

"What happened?" Cici slurred.

One of the boys—I can't remember who was driving the car I was in—got out.

"I've got drink all over me," I pouted.

"It'll be okay," Cici said as she rubbed liquid off my arm as best she could.

The guy finally got back in the car.

"What happened?" I asked.

"Man, they stopped outta nowhere."

"He rear ended him," Andrea spoke clearly. Remember, I told you, she doesn't drink. "Do you need me to drive?" she asked the guy.

"Nah. We good. We'll deal with it later. Let's go!" He turned the music back up and we bumped to it all the way out to the party.

We parked and there were people everywhere. Everyone was dressed in anything but clothes and the party was definitely lit. We were standing in line when I heard B's voice. He was yelling over the music to some people, telling them what direction they needed to go to get in line.

"That's my man," I said to some random girl in front of me with a huge grin on my face.

She looked at me like I was crazy and said 'okay' as she rolled her eyes.

When B spotted me, he smiled and winked then went back to doing his job.

We all got in a little while later and it was packed. The party was held in a huge warehouse and it was the best event I had seen all year.

We were all trying to stick together while we were inside. At one point, I grabbed onto Cici to try and keep up with the group. She turned around quickly.

"Cole, stop! You're pulling on me!"

I don't know if Cici was actually upset with me or if she yelled because the music was so loud. Cici had never yelled at me before, and as intoxicated as I was, her yelling at me was devastating.

"I'm gonna go sit against the wall by the door," I told her as I let go.

I walked over to the wall and sat down, crying.

Again, day drinking is very bad.

All of a sudden, I heard a crash across the room. Things were being thrown and the crowd moved closer to where I was sitting. It was the weirdest feeling; it was as if the crowd was moving like it was being fast-forwarded, but I was moving up the wall in slow motion. I just knew if I didn't stand up fast enough, I would be trampled by the crowd that was swiftly approaching.

I looked to my right and saw a guy standing there next to me. We locked eyes and he reached his arm over toward me to help me get up. Just as I was reaching back out to him, somebody picked me up and carried me outside. I was crying so hard I had no clue who had grabbed me.

I didn't know where my friends were. The space around me was spinning. In my mind, Cici hated me. I almost got stomped on and died. And now, to make matters worse, I had been abducted.

"Are you okay?" The sound was barely audible.

My feet touched the ground.

"Cole? Cole? Are you okay?"

Okay, so this person knew me. Maybe I hadn't been abducted.

"Cole? Open your eyes."

I opened my eyes and realized it was B standing in front of me.

"Are you okay?"

I nodded as tears continued to fall out of my eyes.

He grabbed me and held onto me tightly.

* * *

You would have really thought B cared about me. My safety and well-being *were* important to him. Until they weren't.

One night, Cici asked Andrea and me if we cared if she had a friend over. Andrea and I looked at each other and then back to Cici.

"Why would we care?" I asked.

"Well," she smiled, "he has a friend with him."

I took a swig of my Smirnoff Ice. *Look, I was young, okay. Smirnoff Ice is really good when you're underage and your taste buds haven't matured enough for you to like beer.*

"Don't look at me." I laughed.

Cici turned to Andrea.

"What do you mean?" Andrea looked at me.

"She's asking because the friend of this friend wants another girl to hang out with. I'm all about chilling and drinking, but I've got B, so I'm not the friend Cici needs to be asking." I smirked and took another sip of my drink.

Andrea smiled and looked back to Cici. "I don't care. They can come over."

A little while later, two guys walked into our apartment. We all sat around the table and played cards and drank *draanks*. It was all going pretty well except Andrea was obviously attracted to the other guy, but no matter how hard I tried to get him to focus his attention on her, he kept flirting with me. I was either going to have to be a total bitch or remove myself from the situation.

Cici and her guy went into her room and shut the door before I could get up and leave the group. I finished my drink and started walking toward my room. Andrea followed and the other guy took that as an invitation as well. I lay across my bed and Andrea and the other guy sat on the floor in front of me. The last thing I remember before waking up was laughing and talking to the two of them.

When I woke up, the light in my room was off. Andrea was no longer sitting on the floor and my door was shut. Everything started registering when I felt a hand trying to get inside of my jeans. The other guy was still in my room and he was on my bed, next to me. I looked down and saw my zipper was undone.

"What are you doing?" I asked.

He started kissing on my neck.

"Stop," I whispered.

He stopped kissing my neck, but his hands were still working to get in my pants.

"Stop," I said more aggressively.

For just what I'm sure was a brief second, but what felt like forever, I wrestled his hand out of my pants.

He rolled onto his back and let out a frustrated sigh.

"Can you get out, please?" I raised my voice at him.

He just looked at me but didn't budge.

"Leave!"

He still didn't move.

"Okay, *I'm* leaving."

I got up and zipped up my pants, slipped on my shoes, and walked out of my room. Andrea was coming out of her room.

"What's going on?" she asked.

"Man, she trippin . . ." the other guy said as he followed behind me.

"I would get in your room and lock the door if I were you," I said to Andrea.

The other guy plopped on the couch. I grabbed my keys.

"Where are you going?" Andrea asked.

"I'm going to B's."

"Should you be driving?"

"I'll be fine."

I definitely shouldn't have been driving. I was still a little buzzed, plus I was shaking and freaking out about the fact that a man was just in my room trying to get into my pants without my consent. It was definitely a bad idea.

I called B on my way over but couldn't stop crying as I tried to explain to him what had just happened.

"Cole, get off the phone with me and just tell me when you get here. You need to focus on driving."

I managed to make it to B's safely. I parked my car and walked up to his apartment. We went into his room and the tears flooded as I told him how I had gotten so close to being raped.

"Why was there a guy in your room?"

That's what he asked me.

He didn't get angry at the guy in my room. He didn't ask me how I was feeling or if I was all right.

"Why was there a guy in your room?"

B didn't care if I was okay.

* * *

I COULD GO on and on and back and forth with good stories and bad stories about B. We had laughter and tears, happiness and heartache, and times when we tried really hard to make it work. In the end, we were both at fault, but ultimately our demise started with the cheating.

I remember the day that everything changed, when my love life went from shaky to being completely flipped upside down. I still remember how my stomach dropped and how I went from feeling enraged to feeling absolutely nothing. I became numb. My entire body became numb. An overreaction? Maybe. But I was 21 years old and so deep in love, I had lost myself and I didn't even know it.

"I don't want to tell you because you won't be able to focus on your work," Mitch, my friend-turned-supervisor, told me.

I was working on campus at a retail dining area. The café was closed and it was time for the real work to start. Each of us employees was assigned a specific task and the sooner we got our work done, the sooner we could get the fuck out of there and get to drinking.

I was on floors that night and Mitch was refilling the napkin dispensers. I wasn't the least bit interested in making the floors squeaky clean. I didn't care if we had to stay later. I couldn't go home without knowing what Mitch had to tell me anyway.

"Come on, Mitch. You've had me waiting all shift to hear

what you have to say. We're closing. Come on. Tell me. Please," I begged.

"Yeah, we're closing, but we've still got stuff to do. *You've* got stuff to do. I'll tell you later." He was sitting down at one of the tables, stuffing canisters with napkins.

"I'll still do my work, I swear." I pouted as I stood in front of him with a mop in my hand. "It can't be worse than working all day with this pit in my stomach wondering what it is you're gonna tell me. Come on. I don't mind begging."

He stopped what he was doing and placed the napkins on the table in front of him. His eyes met my pleading ones and he sighed. "You've got to promise me you'll keep doing your work."

I lifted two fingers and held them by my shoulder. "Scout's honor." I put my fingers down. "I swear."

"So, I've got a friend. She asked me a couple of weeks ago if you have a boyfriend. I told her you do, that you're dating B and then I asked why she brought it up. She said she has a friend who has a crush on you, and she wasn't sure if you were dating anyone, but she knew we were friends and worked together."

My brow furrowed, and I wondered why Mitch was making such a big deal about it. I parted my lips to speak, but he continued before I could ask. "I didn't think much about it and never talked to her again about what she'd asked until a couple of days ago."

"Okay," I squeaked. My heart started racing. There was more. I had a feeling where this was going, but I wouldn't let myself believe it.

"She said, 'you know how I asked you about Cole a couple weeks ago?' and I nodded. She then told me, 'well, it wasn't really for a friend. I've actually been dating B on and off for a while and I wanted to know if Cole was really his girlfriend.'" He stopped, and his eyes scanned mine, searching for my reaction to what he'd just said. I didn't give him one. I just stood there, waiting for him to continue.

"So, I asked her what she meant by *a while* and she held up two fingers. I asked her two what? Two weeks, two months? And she just shook her head and whispered 'years.'"

I gulped . . . hard.

There was more to the story. Apparently, the girl had also told Mitch B had traveled to see her over the recent holiday break and had met her grandparents. I guessed who it was, and Mitch confirmed. She had added me on Facebook probably a year prior, but I hadn't thought much of it. The black community on campus was relatively small and most people in the community followed each other on social media platforms. I don't know why my mind automatically went to her, but it did. She had only liked pictures of B and me. I don't know why I had never put two and two together.

I went into the bathroom and sent B a text.

Me: Who is the girl whose grandparents you met in December? The one you went to Milledgeville to see?

I put my phone in my pocket, but it didn't take long for it to vibrate. I pulled it out and unlocked it with shaky hands.

B: Her name is Hillary

The phone vibrated again.

B: And yes, we've had sex.

I almost dropped the phone in the toilet. I pushed back the tears and opened the door. I put the phone back in my pocket and kept my promise to Mitch. I continued doing my work.

* * *

I COULD FILL an entire book with stories about B and there's almost a 100% guarantee that one day, you'll get those stories. But there's not enough pages in this book to tell all of them here. I'll just leave you with knowing B and I didn't work out, and the three years I spent with him were definitely the beginning of The Relationshit Show.

Take that as you will, and get comfortable. You've got fifteen more episodes. Grab your popcorn, some tissues, and of course some wine. Time to binge read your favorite show.

EPISODE 3

⚜

THE SORRY ONE

I met this one when I was a baby. Not a literal baby, but a twenty-one-year-old baby, and of course I thought I was grown. We all do at that age, but the older you get, you realize twenty-one is still a child. An infant.

I was an intern at the place Sorry worked and in a relationship when I met him, so nothing was ever going to happen between us. There was some harmless flirting, but thinking back on it, the stare he gave me—the one I thought was so intense and sexy—was actually pretty creepy. He was thirty-four at the time, so I was infatuated with the idea that a 'grown-up' was interested in me. But, like I said, I was an intern and I was B's girlfriend.

Fast forward six months after meeting him and I was no longer an intern and no longer . . . well, you read the last episode.

I couldn't tell you how Sorry and I exchanged phone numbers. It was too long ago. However, I remember how it all started . . .

One night, I was downtown Athens with a couple of my friends. We drank and danced and laughed and had a good time. After having some whiskey that made me frisky, I decided I wanted to go over to Sorry's apartment. He lived right down the street, and we had been texting all night, and I was still heartbroken over B. Seemed like a good idea, right?

My friends dropped me off and after making sure Sorry met me by the gate, they pulled away. Sorry and I went upstairs and he showed me around. His roommate wasn't home, so we chilled in the living room. One thing led to another and soon I was on the couch without a shirt on, and Sorry was giving me that intense stare he had given me every day I saw him when I interned.

We moved to his bedroom and you might think you know what happened next. Trust me, you don't.

There was a lot of apologizing and almost insertions. I got dick-tapped on my inner thighs a couple of times. Faces were made like some really intense fucking was happening, but there wasn't. I lay on my back, spread eagle, watching it all happen above me.

I rushed out of there as quickly as I could the next morning because I had to take my friend Marsha to the doctor. Seriously . . . it wasn't an excuse. The night before, she had asked me if I could take her to the doctor and I'd told her I would.

Sorry dropped me off at my apartment. Once inside, I promptly showered and threw on some bum clothes before heading over to Marsha's to pick her up. I called her when I got there. A few minutes later, she was in the car and off we went.

"So . . ." Marsha nudged my shoulder. "How was last night?" She had a huge grin on her face.

"You don't want to know."

She laughed. "Of course I do. That's why I asked."

"Nope. Trust me. You don't. I'm never going back."

Marsha laughed again.

While we were in the waiting room at the doctor's office, I told Marsha *what had happened was*. She couldn't stop laughing.

"Are you serious?" she asked.

"Yes! And then he said, 'I don't normally do this.'"

"What do you think he meant by that?"

"I don't know. 'I don't normally fuck like this' or 'I don't normally fuck at all'—I couldn't tell you! But I will tell you one thing, I am never doing that again."

I lied.

Of course, I did it again.

It got better over time. The sex, not the situationship. Situationship was not a term in circulation when Sorry and I started doing what we did, but that's what it was. A situationship is defined as "a relationship that has no label on it… like a friendship, but more than a friendship, but not quite a relationship." It's a real thing. Seriously. I just googled it and that description in quotes popped up on UrbanDictionary.com.

We talked and hung out, and whatever it was we did caused the ultimate end to my relationship with B. You don't know what I'm talking about, but if I land another publishing deal—that is, if this book is actually published and doesn't just sit on my computer—I will tell the entire story of B and me and you'll understand that little nugget right there. It wasn't my fault. I swear. We're best friends (yeah, you, the person reading this, and me), so you can trust me.

Anyhoo . . . let's dive into some stories.

* * *

FOR SOME ODD REASON, Sorry had a thing for asking me how Marsha was doing. Yes, they eventually met when we were all out one night. He talked to all my friends and all of my friends liked him. It was one reason why he was so appealing there for a while because B was never really into my friends. He would say hey, but then walk right past them. They didn't like him. He didn't like them. So, when Sorry was really great with my friends, I was super into it.

So, yeah, every time I'd see Sorry, he'd ask, 'How's Marsha?' And he'd always ask in a tone that sounded a little Matthew McConaughey mixed with creepy as fuck. I don't know if he was genuine with his question, or if he was into Marsha, or if he knew it bugged the shit out of me, so that's why he asked literally every single time I saw him.

One weekend I was in Athens visiting Marsha. It was after I had graduated from college and I was living back at home with my mom. While I was in town, I was going to go out on a date with Sorry. He came to Marsha's to pick me up and I wasn't quite ready. He stayed downstairs while I ran upstairs to finish my makeup.

The date went pretty well. We went to some Thai spot. I had never had Thai food before, but had been willing to give it a try. I'll try just about anything once. The food was okay, but I probably wouldn't choose it again. The conversation was better, and we got along just as well as we normally had.

After the date, he dropped me back off at Marsha's. I went inside and put my leftover food in the fridge.

"I have some leftover food if you want it," I said to Marsha after I crashed on the futon. "Sorry wanted to make sure I brought some back for you." I rolled my eyes, laughing.

"He what?" she asked.

"He had leftover food and told me to put it in my to-go box for you."

"You know he invited me on y'all's date?"

I sat up straight. "What?"

Marsha laughed. "Yeah. While you were upstairs finishing

getting ready, he asked me if I had any plans and when I said no, he told me I should go with you guys."

"Are you kidding me?"

"Nope."

* * *

SORRY AND I continued talking for a while. Back and forth. On and off. I invited him to be my date to a wedding once and he turned me down.

"I just think that's what couples do," he said.

I thought 'talking' for months on end would eventually lead us to a relationship, but it never did. He pushed me away and eventually all the back and forth, on and off, led to nowhere.

We ended up working together again after I got a job at the place where I'd interned . . . the place where he worked . . . the place where I met him. When it comes to my day job, I'm very professional. I don't let my personal life affect my work life, and I never let things get awkward. A coworker who pretty much knew the gist of Sorry's and my former relationship, once told me, 'I would never guess you two had history'.

Good. That's how I wanted it.

Things were cordial between us, but I wasn't his biggest fan. I tolerated him. There were some things done and said that he couldn't take back, but this next story takes the cake.

Some coworkers had planned a get together for some reason or another. I can't remember what it was for, but I do know we were in the party room at one of the taco places in town. Sorry was there and we said our 'hellos', but that was it. We sat at different tables and talked to different people.

Toward the end of dinner, he came to the table where I was sitting at and struck up a conversation. We were around coworkers, so normal and not awkward, remember? I spoke back and answered his questions and then, finally, the dinner was over.

One of my good friends from work, Taylor, said she was meeting her roommate upstairs for trivia. I told her I would join her soon, but I was going to grab another drink from the bar. Our other good friend, Isaiah, said he was gonna sit with me at the bar, and for some reason, he invited Sorry to join us. Isaiah looked at me and laughed as I glared at him for asking. He knew the history there, but he liked Sorry and he loved torturing me, in a little brother sort of way.

The three of us went upstairs and sat at the bar. We ordered drinks and talked for a little bit before Taylor called me and told me to come sit with her and her roommate and her roommate's friends to help them with trivia. I told her Sorry and Isaiah were with me, and she said there was plenty of room. We headed over there and my unwanted night with Sorry continued. It was pretty uneventful, but still . . .

We went to another bar and Taylor's roommate, Jenny, and I exchanged numbers. She was cool people and I was all about making new girl friends in Athens. We seemed to have a good bit in common and we both enjoyed a good drink. Or two. Or five. She also told me Sorry was following me around like a puppy dog after she asked who he was. I laughed when she said that, and I decided I liked her.

There was one weekend Jenny and I decided to meet up to drink downtown for the night. Taylor was working or was out of town so she couldn't join us. It was going to just be me and Jenny, but I thought we got along well enough that we'd be okay without the mutual friend buffer.

I had texted Jenny earlier in the day to ask her what time she wanted to meet. I knew she had a date with a guy she had met on a dating site, so I thought maybe she wanted to meet right after their date. They were eating downtown after all.

Jenny: So . . . I have something to tell you.
Me: What is it?
Jenny: My date is actually with Sorry. I really did run across him on the dating app, but yeah, it's him.
Me: Okay. That's fine. I wouldn't date him, but you do you. Seriously, it doesn't bother me.

It really didn't. I had no claim on him and if she wanted to fall into that trap, that was on her.

Jenny: Well, I kind of invited him to go out with us afterward.
Me: Uuuuuh. Does he know you're going out with me?
Jenny: Yeah. Please don't be mad.

Okay. So, I'm totally cool if she wants to date the man, but *I* don't want to hang out with him. I'm not his biggest fan, remember? What was I to do? She had already invited him.

Me: It wouldn't be my first choice to hang out with him, but you've already invited him so . . . what time?

I got to the bar early that night. When we went out that summer, we usually started at the bar that served the slushy drinks. That bar was typically where all the underage kids went, so the trick was to get there at the beginning of the night before they all showed up, get your slushy drink, and bounce.

I sat at the bar and the bartender who usually worked the early shift came over and started talking to me.

"Hey, girl! What can I get ya? Alone tonight?"

"No, just early and I need a drink."

She laughed. "Uh oh. What's going on? I can tell something's wrong."

I leaned in on the bar. "So, you know the girl with the shorter blonde hair that I usually come in with?"

"Yeah."

"Well, I'm meeting her and she's bringing a date."

"Third wheelin' it?"

"Yeah, but that's not the problem. Her date is someone I used to talk to. Like you could pretty much consider him an ex."

The bartender's eyes grew wide. "And she knows this?"

"Yes! And she asked if it was okay that she'd asked him to join us. What was I supposed to say? She had already asked him!"

"Awkward . . ."

"RIGHT?"

"So, what do you want to drink? It's on the house."

I was starting on drink number two when Jenny and Sorry walked into the bar. The bar was pretty much empty. The only occupants were me, the employees, and a guy all the way at the far end of the bar. Of all the different seating arrangements that could have happened, any of them would have been better than what actually happened.

Jenny sat in the empty seat to my left. Instead of following Jenny and sitting on her other side, Sorry came in, said hey to me and then proceeded to sit in the empty seat to my right. I was smack dab in the middle of them. How did this happen? I sucked down my drink and looked at the bartender. She shook her head, snickered, and started making my third before she asked Jenny and Sorry what they wanted to drink.

Some of my other friends eventually showed up and made things less awkward. In the larger crowd, I wasn't stuck between Jenny and Sorry all night. At one point, Jenny complained to me about how Sorry was on his phone the entire time they were eating dinner earlier and how she was pretty sure some girl kept calling him.

Insert shoulder shrug emoji.

At the end of the night, the whole group traveled to the local Italian pizzeria to grab some slices of huge, greasy, delicious pizza. It was crowded like it typically was for the hour, but we didn't stand in line long. Some of the guys walked over to the 24-hour diner down the street, while Jenny, Sorry, two of the other girls, and I stayed at the pizza place.

I ordered my slice and as I was waiting for my number to be called, I realized I didn't have my things. Things, as in my cell phone and my wallet. I asked the girls if I had handed them my stuff. They all started looking through their purses, but no luck. I asked Sorry, who was already sitting in a booth, chowing down on some pizza, if he'd seen my stuff. Nope. I had just ordered and paid for my food, so it had to be somewhere, right?

My number was called. I grabbed my pizza and decided I would look for my things after I was done eating. I was drunk and I was starving. I sat across from Sorry and started eating my pizza. I was about halfway done with my slice of pepperoni with feta when my things suddenly appeared in front of me on the table. And by magically *appeared* in front of me, I mean Sorry pulled them out from behind him and placed them on the table.

"You need to be more responsible."

I put my slice of pizza down and looked up at Sorry. I only saw the features of his face for a brief moment before I saw red. And no, my eyes were not glazed with marinara sauce. I was livid. I only remember saying 'excuse me?' before Sorry repeated himself and then started to speak to me like I was his child.

Red turned to a raging black and the next thing I knew, we were on the street and I was flicking off Sorry with a big

FUCK YOU. I came back to reality when I told him never to speak to me again and to walk away. Some more *fuck you*s flew and hit him in the face until finally he turned around and starting walking in the direction of his apartment.

I walked to the 24-hour diner where everyone else had since gone. I found my friends and plopped down in a seat.

"Are you okay?" one of the girls asked.

"Yeah, I'm good."

"Jenny said you and Sorry were really going at it."

I looked up at Jenny. I hadn't been mad at her before, but in that moment, I wasn't sure if I should be angry with her for bringing Sorry around or happy that she did because clearly I needed to get some things off my chest.

"It's all good," I said.

I looked at the table and saw plates piled with fries. That's when I realized I hadn't even finished my pizza. The guy next to me looked over and saw me staring, probably with a mouthwatering glare on my face.

He laughed and held up a french fry and tapped me on the nose. "You want one?"

* * *

LIKE I SAID BEFORE, Sorry and I worked together, so I was bound to run into him again. Silence was still cordial right? I didn't have anything to say to him after that night. In our respective positions, we didn't see each other much, but when we did, I usually went the opposite direction.

Eventually there was an event we both had to work and we were paired up. Funny how those kinds of things happen. We talked a little bit, but it was superficial and neither one of us touched on the subject of what had happened that night in the middle of the street. The silent treatment once again became sincere cordiality, but I knew we could never hang out outside of work again. Shockingly, he asked me out a few times after that and I turned him down.

One day, I needed to come in late to work. Sorry was the lucky one who had to cover my position while I was out. I got to work in time to eat lunch, so I dropped my things off at my desk and went into the breakroom for a few minutes to eat with some of my friends, and then I went back out to my desk.

Now, most people aren't huge fans of sitting at my desk, so once I get there to take over, they're chomping at the bit to get up and go. Sorry, however, saw me coming to the desk and remained in the seat. I mentally rolled my eyes and willed him to please let any semblance of a friendship go and just get up and leave.

Thank you for covering the desk, but go. Please.

He started his usual small talk with me.

"How's it going?" he asked.

"Pretty good. Can't complain."

"How's Marsha?"

I rolled my eyes out loud this time. "She's good."

I'm not sure what else we talked about, between the casual conversation and the crying. Yes, you read that correctly. Crying.

If you were wondering why Sorry has been called Sorry the entire time you've been reading this episode, you're about to find out. I didn't call this man Sorry because he's a sorry individual, which you may have guessed from the whole *stealing my things to make me feel like an irresponsible child* bit, but no. That wasn't it.

I won't get into everything he said to me because I just don't feel comfortable sharing his story. How he treated me and the things he did to me are mine. Those incidents are a part of my story. The journey Sorry had to go on to discover what's inside of him is his story. It's for him to tell, not me.

That day, at that desk, Sorry apologized. He simply said sorry for everything he did to me, for pushing me away, and for his behavior toward me. He cried about it. This man, at forty-one years old, was crying to me because he was truly sorry for how he had treated me in the past. I accepted his apology, but I felt nothing. It was too little too late, but I appreciated the gesture. At that point, I feel like it was something he needed more than I did. I was already over the pain and the anger. I was numb toward him. However, out of all the men you'll read about here, he is the only one who has ever apologized to me and that, I guess, is worth a thank you.

EPISODE 4

THE DJ

*O*kay, *Journal, I just had the weirdest fucking night of my life. And I'm not saying that to be punny because there was some fucking. So, I'm not trying to say the weirdest fucking night of my life, because who really has a "fucking night"? Like a night for fucking? Is that a thing? And if it is, would it really be weird? Or maybe people are into that sort of thing. Which is cool. No judgement here.*

What I'm trying to get at is that I just had the weirdest. fucking. night. *where I got fucked.*

So, me and Biff were at this party in Atlanta. There were a bunch of her friends from college and it was at some random house. I had no clue where I was, but Biff did so *shrug*.

Of course drinks were had, and I was feeling a little tipsy. Okay, okay, a lotta tipsy. Somehow, we found our way upstairs. In my alcohol-induced state, this dreamboat of a man almost ran into me in the small, cramped hallway. We locked eyes and just stared at one another. He smiled at me and I swear, I almost melted onto the floor right there. Into a puddle of lust.

Biff totally saw what was going on and had a sly grin on

her face as that man—we'll call him Babe—walked past me. His hand touched my shoulder and heat coursed through my body to my very special place. I immediately pushed through the crowd toward Biff and whisper-yelled to her that Babe was so cute and I wanted to fuuuuuuck. It was probably the alcohol talking—you know, liquid courage and all—*and* the fact that I did not expect Biff to do what she did next.

She walked over to Babe, grabbed him by the arm, and whispered something into his ear that I could not hear over all the music and chatter. Then she turned around and started walking toward me with that huge grin still on her face.

I asked her what she'd said to him and she said, and I quote, "If you two don't stop staring at each other and just go fuck, I'm going to take her downstairs. You have sixty seconds." Biff quickly said 'you're welcome' to me as I felt the same heat begin to crawl down my arm. Babe had approached without me realizing it and grabbed me, pulling me into a room across the hall and shutting the door right behind us.

I asked him if we were supposed to be in there and he told me it was his room and that Biff told him I wanted him. Immediately, without letting me say a thing, he pulled down his basketball shorts, along with his boxers, and stared at me with a mischievous look on his face.

How I noticed his face, I wasn't sure, because below it was a very hard dick. A beautiful, large, chocolate penis. I was in my happy place.

My mouth hung open and I couldn't utter a single word. I guess Babe took the look on my face and the fact that I sat down on the bed while I was still staring at his junk as a 'yeah, let's do this'.

His smile grew larger and he stepped out of the shorts that had dropped to the floor.

"Uh uh." He shook his head, sat down on a chair shaped like the palm of a hand, and began stroking himself. "Come here."

I smirked like the smirking emoji and pulled my shirt off before stumbling over toward where Babe was waiting for me. I'm sure in my head I thought I was walking over toward him like a feline about to pounce on its prey, but I'm even more positive it was not like that at all. However it happened, I ended up exactly where I wanted to be.

Minutes passed and more clothes scattered. We moved from the hand . . . it was the chair, remember . . . to the bed, to the floor, and at last, to the bed again. It was great sex and I was so grateful to Biff for essentially calling my bluff.

We got dressed and opened the door. Babe walked out and immediately started hyping the party back up. It was starting to die down, and I guess he couldn't let that happen to an event going on at his house.

I looked across the hall and Biff was standing against a wall looking at me while also on the verge of laughter. I made my way over to her and asked if I needed to fix anything as I brushed my hair out of my face.

"No, woman. You look fine. So, how was it? Tell me! I need to know."

"It was good." I couldn't give her all the details. But now that I think about it, I totally could have because I'm sharing it now with the world . . . well, whoever ends up reading this hot mess express of a book. I guess I didn't give you ALL the details, did I? But I did end up telling Biff eventually. We've known each other for almost twenty years. I'm bound to tell her everything, whether she wants to know it or not. And here I am getting off track again. Let's go back to the conversation.

"Mmmmhmmm. Suuure, it was just good. Was he big? I've always wondered."

"Wait. You know him?" I asked.

"Uhm, yes, girl. He went to [an all-male school in Atlanta that I'm not going to name]. I've known him for years. You really think I'd walk up to some rando and tell him to take you into a room and fuck you?"

"Good point." I nodded.

"So? Was it big?"

I laughed a little. "I would say it was average. It wasn't huge, but it was definitely a good size and he definitely knew how to use it." I blushed, living over the moments again in my head.

"I knew it. He looks like it would be average. Well at least it was good. You're welcome."

And that's where it all started.

Babe became the guy I hooked up with most times I was in Atlanta for the weekend. House parties, kickbacks, bars— it always went down between us. We were like two rabbits that just couldn't help it.

One night, Biff and I were out bar hopping in Edgewood. We walked past some place that was playing some pretty good music.

"I wanna go in there," I remember telling Biff as we walked to our usual spot where we started off our nights of draanks.

"Babe is DJing in there tonight," she stated matter of factly.

So, I haven't shared with you all, but I had discovered that Babe was a local DJ. He hosted all kinds of parties and booked all kinds of gigs. It was his thing. At 23 or 24 or whatever his age—early twenties?—I thought that was an awesome job and I found it sexy as fuck. Super successful at what he loved, and he was good at it. Yeah, it turned me on.

"He's what?" I grabbed Biff by her arm and stopped her in the middle of the sidewalk.

Of course, there were some creepers standing against the brick wall looking us up and down.

"Hey, ladies." One of them lifted himself up off the wall and started walking toward us.

"Yeah, girl. Come on. We'll come back." Biff glared at the guy coming toward us. "No, thank you."

After we grabbed a couple of drinks at our typical first stop and after Biff had text Babe to confirm he was still DJing at that other spot, we headed back to the bar with The DJ.

"He asked if you were with me." Biff laughed as we walked arm in arm down the street.

"Did he now?" I asked.

Biff simply nodded her head.

As soon as we walked in, I saw Babe up in the DJ booth. He was dishing out music like Waffle House dishes out food to drunk people at 2 a.m. The building was filled with sweaty bodies swaying back and forth to the beat. We could hear people talking about nonsense or ordering food through the little hole in the wall to the kitchen.

Biff texted him when we arrived. It only took a few seconds before Babe looked at his phone, then looked down into the crowd and locked eyes with me. We smiled at each other and that was all it took. He whispered something to one of the other people in the booth, he said something into the mic to rile up the crowd, the music got louder and Babe jumped down from where he was.

Some other friends had joined Biff and me on the dance floor. When Babe made it to our group, he very quickly said hello to everyone, but promptly grabbed me by the arm. "Come on."

He pushed our way through the crowd and for a split second I felt like a celebrity by association. Everyone seemed to know Babe and I was getting looks of excitement and glares of jealousy as we made our way through the room.

Eventually Babe found the door he was looking for. He pushed it open, and just like the first night we met, he pulled me inside. Once the door shut behind us, he grabbed the back of my neck and pulled my face toward his. When his lips met mine, he kissed me with so much passion, my knees buckled.

Babe turned me around and lifted my skirt before I heard the zipper of his jeans. My eyes finally adjusted, and I realized we were in a storage closet. As was typical for us, I asked him if we were supposed to be in there. He told me he knew the guy who owned the place and that it was fine. I had never fucked in a public place before and it was thrilling. I was even more turned on than I had ever been with him before.

He put his hand in the middle of my back and pushed me over so I was leaning against something in the dark. I didn't care what it was, I just wanted him inside of me. I didn't have to wait long before he was thrusting in and out of me like a wild animal. What did I tell you? Rabbits.

It was the first time I had been with someone where all I wanted to do was have sex. There was nothing there beyond that. I didn't want to be with him. I knew we would never work and I was okay with that. I felt empowered and sexy and I was in control of my body and getting what I wanted, and I wasn't ashamed of that.

After knocking over who-knows-what in the closet, I pushed my skirt back down, smoothing out any wrinkles. He lifted his pants back into place and kissed me once more. When we tried to open the door, something was blocking it from opening.

"Are we stuck in here?" I asked with slurred words. The drinks from the pregame and the first bar were finally catching up.

"We better not be. I need to get back up to the booth." He shoved at the door. "Help me."

I rolled my eyes and began pushing on the door with him. Slowly but surely, we got the door open enough for us to squeeze through. When I finally made it to the other side, I noticed somebody had moved a couch in front of the door. Two girls were sitting on it and gave me the bitchiest looks I've ever received when we made eye contact. Judgement glossed over their eyes. I gave them a bitchy smile back and a two-finger wave before I shut the door behind me and made it back over to my group of friends.

Biff shook her head and laughed. "You naughty, naughty girl."

I joined in the laughter and we danced the rest of the night away.

* * *

MONTHS PASSED and I didn't see Babe out. We didn't communicate when we weren't fucking, so I had kind of forgotten about him.

I was at Biff's house one night and we couldn't think of anything fun to do. We were drinking vodka in the kitchen when she mentioned one of her friends from college was in town for the weekend. She hadn't seen him in ages and thought maybe he would want to come over and chill with us.

"He's friends with Babe."

My eyes grew larger as his name struck a chord somewhere inside of me.

"Babe . . . I haven't heard from him in forever."

"I know. He told me he's pretty sure you're mad at him."

I took a sip of the vodka soda sitting in front of me. "Why would I be mad at him?"

Biff shrugged her shoulders. "Something about owing you money." She raised an eyebrow and stared at me, waiting for an explanation.

See, I had never told Biff that Babe and I had had an *uh-oh*. We were very careful to use protection every time we had sex, but there was this one time when we both were extremely hammered and horny and the condom just didn't make it on before we were joined together. I was on birth control, but we decided to take an extra step to ensure there were no babies.

I told him I would pay for the Plan B up front and he told me he would give me his half the next time I saw him. I don't know what your views are on birth control or family planning and all of that—and this book is not going to get into that discussion—but I know we can all agree that when you are fresh out of college, working a job that pays you nowhere close to what you need to earn to survive out of your parents' house, fifty dollars is a lot of money. Not getting the twenty-five dollars you deserve in return for covering the fifty dollars is a total bitch.

I had seen Babe a total of two times since I'd bought the thing and both of those times he did not give me what I was owed. One of those times, we hooked up. Animals, I'm telling you.

I took another sip of my drink and just smiled at Biff.

"Well, does he owe you money?"

"Yeah. Twenty-five dollars, but I've already accepted the fact that I'm not gonna get that back."

"So, you're not mad at him?" she asked.

I shrugged my shoulders. "It's whatever."

"Do you care if he comes over?"

"What?" I asked, confused.

"Random Friend from College is with him." I can't think of what Random Friend from College's name actually was and I don't feel like making one up. He only gets mentioned like one other time in this episode, so it doesn't really matter. You shouldn't get too confused. "They want to come over. Do you care?"

The rest of my drink magically disappeared down my throat. "Nah. I don't care. That's fine."

Biff laughed. "You know he's not going to have your twenty-five dollars with him."

"I told you, already accepted." I slid my way over to the freezer and grabbed the half empty bottle of vodka out of it.

Not long after my plastic cup was refilled, the doorbell rang. Biff ran to answer the door while I stayed in the kitchen. I was leaned on the counter, my cup to my lips, when Babe walked through the kitchen door.

"What's up?" he asked with a smug grin on his face.

I swallowed the liquid that sat in my mouth and simply gave him a head nod. Before I could say anything, Biff and the random friend from college came waltzing into the kitchen.

Biff introduced us. "Cole, this is Random Friend from College. Random Friend from College, this is Cole."

"What's good?" he asked as he reached his hand out toward me for me to shake.

Again, I gave a gentle head nod, but I let this one have my hand.

Biff and Random Friend from College struck up a conversation about something while she poured him a drink.

From the time he stepped into the kitchen, Babe kept his eyes on me. I continued to sip at my drink and I simply stared back at him. He glanced up at Biff.

"Yo, is there somewhere I could go talk to Cole?"

Biff stopped talking and quickly looked at me. I shrugged my shoulders, letting her know it was okay. Unsure if he really wanted to just talk to me or if we were gonna end up doing what it is we always did, Biff directed us to the empty room upstairs. One of her roommates had moved out, so there was a room upstairs with literally only carpet on the floor.

He reached his hand out. "Will you come with me?"

I stared at his hand, took a sip of my drink, and looked back up to his face.

"Please?" he urged.

My eyes made their way back to his hand. I had grabbed that hand so many times. It led me to lands of bliss and hot, steamy, inappropriate sex. For some reason, I thought he was serious about wanting to talk to me. Part of me hoped he wasn't. Part of me wanted what we always had: good sex and nothing else. That's what Babe gave me, so why was I so upset about twenty-five dollars?

We made it to the room and he shut the door behind us. He asked me how I was doing and attempted more small talk before grabbing onto my hand again. He pulled me toward him and started kissing me. Shockingly, I pushed him away after we kissed for what seemed like far too long. I realized I wasn't drunk enough for this shit. And Babe wasn't drunk at all, so what was the kiss for?

I walked out of the room and I heard him laugh quietly before following me downstairs. Once we were back in the kitchen, the four of us talked and continued drinking. While we were talking, I noticed half of Babe's left ear lobe was missing. It was gone. Seriously. How had I not noticed this in the months we had been fucking? Oh yeah . . . alcohol.

"What happened to your ear?" I asked him.

He automatically reached up and touched his lobe . . . or lack thereof.

"I used to wrestle in high school." He put his hand back by his side.

"Okay . . . and?" I probed for more of an explanation.

"Accident on the mat," he said as he shrugged his shoulders.

Clearly, I wasn't getting more of the story, so I drank what was left in the cup. My phone vibrated on the counter and I picked up. There was a text from Babe.

Babe: Come upstairs with me.

I looked up at him and smiled while I shook my head. Biff and I hadn't been talking for too long when my phone vibrated again.

Babe: Please. I wanna fuck you sober. I really like you.

Well then. *I* wasn't sober anymore and I was horny. We could deal with the liking me thing later.

Me: Come on.

* * *

I DIDN'T REALLY TALK to Babe much more after that night. At another house party, I tried to pull our usual move: find a room and go at it. After being outside talking to some folks and drinking, I found him walking down the stairs. He hadn't responded to my texts, so I grabbed onto his arm and whispered in his ear to come back up the stairs.

"No," he said.

I furrowed my brows. "What you mean, no?"

"Can't do it."

"And just why not?"

"Biff told me I couldn't have sex with you anymore."

With that, he shrugged out of my grasp and went into the living room to hype up the party. I found Biff and told her what Babe had said and she told me she had definitely not told him that. I didn't talk to Babe after that or see him again.

* * *

THIS PAST SUMMER while I was in Atlanta celebrating my birthday, I got the bright idea to text the number I had for Babe. It was in my phone under "Babe Biff Homecoming." It had been at least two years since I'd spoken to him, but I was drunk and figured why not?

Me: Is this Babe?
Babe: Yes
Babe: [big eyes emoji]
Me: It's Cole
Me: What you up to?
Babe: Hey boo
Babe: At my house wyd
Me: I'm in Buckhead
Me: Tryna figure out what the next move is
Babe: You coming over here [sticking out tongue emoji]
Me: Where's here?
Babe: My house
Me: Why don't you come to the hotel?
Babe: You have a hotel?
Babe: By yourself?
Me: I have a hotel
Me: I'm sharing with my friend but she cool
Babe: Lol what that mean
Me: Like you can come if you want
Me: Or we can come where you at

. . . and he never responded. I should have just asked for my twenty-five dollars.

EPISODE 5

✥

THE COWORKER

*T*here was this one time I worked in a warehouse. It was right after college and I was waiting to get a job at the place where I'd interned, but I needed some money in the meantime. The warehouse was part of the bookstore at the university closer to my mom's house.

Interesting fact: I found out later, I only got hired there because the manager looked me up on Facebook and thought I was hot.

Money is money I guess.

The job was pretty simple. Unload deliveries off big trucks. Tag items. Enter them into the computer. Get them to the bookstore. Store the leftovers. I think that's what we were supposed to be doing.

Anyway, Coworker was hot. He was tall, had big feet, and had a killer smile. We got along right away, and I don't know if it was because he liked my ass or if I liked the bulge in his basketball shorts. Or maybe our personalities just meshed really well. I couldn't tell you what it was, but we became fast friends.

Soon after I started working there, Coworker's cousin

joined the team. His cousin, who we'll call Carrot, also liked my ass and I also liked the bulge in his basketball shorts, so we also got along.

The three of us decided to hang out one night. Now, I'm going to stop you before you get ahead of things. Current fact about me: Never had a threesome.

I mean, I went through my Ho Phase—we all do—but I would never fuck with family. At least not at the same time.

My mom was out of town, so I invited the guys over for a chill night of drinking.

I know my mom is reading this, even though I told her not to, so surprise! Yes, this happened, but look, nothing was broken, I was of age to drink, and nobody got pregnant. Insert super cheesy smiley face emoji.

I invited Biff over as well. In fact, Biff is the reason the cousin got the name Carrot. It makes more sense and is funnier if you know his real name, but Biff was so drunk she called him Carrot while we were all laughing about something. The name stuck. I still talk to Carrot and I will, on occasion, call him Carrot.

While the guys were over, someone (read: probably me) suggested we should play drunken hide and seek in the dark. The game started out pretty fun, but the ending was *really* fun. Coworker and I hooked up for the first time and it was mediocre. But it was sex, and he had a decent sized dick, so it was fun nonetheless.

* * *

COWORKER and I talked on and off for probably less than two months. It was never anything serious, but I liked him, and I thought he was cool people.

He wasn't.

One night, he invited me over to his apartment. It was

pretty late, but I thought 'what the hay? I've got nothing better to do.' I figured I would go over there, we'd hook up, I'd get a little shut eye, and then head back home in the morning. My mom had this rule when I was living with her: she didn't need to know what I was doing or who I was with, I just needed to tell her if I was going to be home for the night. I knew my mom wouldn't get the message until the morning (it was late, remember, and by late, I mean early morning. Like, after two but before five early morning) but I texted her and let her know I was going to be out for the night and I'd be home in the morning.

I got to Coworker's apartment and we went straight to the room. We chilled for a little bit, talking, but we both knew where things were headed. Trust me, what I said next was relevant to the conversation, but I just can't remember what we were talking about.

"I've never watched porn before."

"Really?" he asked.

"For real, I haven't." I laughed.

"Why?"

I shrugged my shoulders. "I don't know. It's just never been something I've thought about doing."

Coworker laughed. He picked up his remote and pressed some buttons and *voilà*, porn appeared on his television. It was super cheesy, and it didn't *really* turn me on, but I was turned on enough to have sex with him. We hooked up and then I curled up under the covers.

Coworker turned over, partially pulling the covers off me. "Well, I need to go to sleep."

"Okay, cool." I grabbed some of the covers back.

"I've got to get up in a few hours for church." He took the covers back.

I sat up in the bed. "Are you kicking me out?"

"Church. In a few hours. Church. Need sleep."

I guess he thought bringing up church so many times was going to make me feel better about being kicked out of bed. Like, who could argue with church, right?

I grabbed my stuff and walked out the door. I sent my mom a text and conversed back with myself since she was still asleep and had never responded to the initial text I sent.

Me: *Nevermind. I'm coming home. I'll be in the house when you wake up.*

* * *

NOT LONG AFTER THAT NIGHT, I was chilling with Carrot at the warehouse. At some point during that conversation, I found out Coworker had a girlfriend.

"I thought you knew," Carrot said.

"Nah. I'm not like that."

Another fact about the author: I don't fuck with family and I don't fuck with guys who have girlfriends or wives.

I don't think I talked to Coworker again. I'm not sure how he's doing or where he's at, but I have faith that fuckboys will be fuckboys.

EPISODE 6

THE OG

*H*e was the definition of tall, dark, and handsome.

I was working at a major department store after college. The place where I had interned while I was in school wanted to hire me, but didn't have an open position available by the time I got that college degree. Of course, not being in school anymore and having to pay off those loans, I needed a job while I waited.

Those extra checks are nice when you're in school. They're real nice until you realize you have to pay the lender back. Every semester that check would come in and I'd be like, 'Oooo, money! How much am I gonna have left over after books and supplies for booze?'

After college, I really wished I had put the leftovers into savings so I'd have had something to start paying off those loans. They give you that grace period so your ass can get a job, but that thing ends really quick.

While I was waiting for that position to open up, I moved back in with my mom like most college graduates do, and not only did I work at the warehouse, I also snagged the job at the department store working loss prevention. Yeah, I was the one who caught people shoplifting. And I was damn good at my job, but that's beside the point.

I remember the first time I saw him. I was sitting in the office, watching the cameras, when he came into view in the men's shoe department. He was tall. He was dark. He was so, so very handsome. His body was lean and he was wearing a blue button-up with khakis and tennis shoes. His smile was everything and it lit up the screen as soon as he started laughing at whatever it was the guy talking to him was saying. I couldn't keep my eyes off him. Until I had to. Someone started to stuff t-shirts into a shopping bag on the screen next to the one he was on.

As weeks went on, I finally stopped watching him on screen like a real creep and introduced myself to him . . . in person. We exchanged numbers. The texting at work was flirty and I was definitely feeling what he was putting out.

I eventually heard back from the job in Athens and would be leaving soon. The two of us decided to hang out outside of work before I left that job and moved back to Athens.

He invited me over to his apartment for drinks and a movie. This was before the whole #netflixandchill thing, so he texted me and actually asked if I wanted to have some drinks and watch a movie.

On my way over, I thought I'd be more nervous than I was. We had spoken quite a bit at work and had texted back and forth, but those interactions were definitely not the same as hanging out, in person, without the distraction of doing our jobs. However, the nerves just weren't there, but all the excitement was.

I parked the car and knocked on the door. It didn't take long for him to answer. He already had a drink in his hand. That smile that I fell for spread across his face and then, there were the nerves. I tried my best to not let them pour out of my fingertips, but they were trying desperately to escape.

I'm getting that feeling of nervousness right now, as I type this. Yeah, he had that kind of effect on me.

After inviting me in, he asked if I wanted what he was having. Whiskey with a splash of ginger ale. I told him I would love a glass. He pointed me toward his bedroom and told me to look in the cabinet his TV was sitting on and pick out a movie.

Before entering his room, I glanced quickly into the living room. No TV. I wondered if the whole 'go into my room' line was just his way of trying to get me in his bed quicker. But there wasn't a television in the living room. Although, there could be a reason the only TV was in his room and the only place to sit in his room was on his bed.

Without any more thoughts to distract me, I walked into the room and placed my purse on the floor. I sat on the floor in front of the cabinet and opened it up to search for just the right movie. I was looking for something that would be interesting enough just in case the sparks weren't there, but not so interesting just in case they were.

Then a cover caught my eye: *The Wolf of Wall Street* starring Leonardo DiCaprio. I snatched it out of the cabinet. I had been dying to see that film. I didn't care if the sparks were there or not; I was going to watch that movie.

"I see you found one." He laughed and headed toward the bed. He placed both cups on the floor and walked back over to where I sat.

"Yes!" I grinned with all my teeth, like a child in a candy store whose parents said she could get one of everything.

He laughed again and took the movie out of my hand.

"All right. Well I guess we're watching my man Leo." He started taking the plastic wrap off the case.

I hadn't noticed it was a brand-new DVD.

"Have you seen it yet?" I asked, getting off the floor.

"Yeah, it's really good. That's why I bought it." He reached his hand out to help me. I took his hand even though I was essentially already off the floor.

Sparks.

"Thanks."

"I think you'll like it." He smirked, clearly feeling what I just felt run through his fingers.

I walked over toward the bed as he finished unwrapping the DVD.

If you're old enough, you'll remember how long that could take and how hard it could be. I don't know if they still do, but there used to be that sticky plastic right at the seam of the case. It's a bitch to get off. And if you were lucky, someone in the factory felt sorry enough for people to put that fucker only on one end. If the factory worker or robot or whoever or whatever was responsible wanted to ruin your day, that shit was on the top and the bottom.

"Thanks for the drink," I said.

"I remember you saying you were a brown liquor girl. Did I do good?"

"So far, you're doing great."

He put the DVD in and the previews started to play. I stood awkwardly by the bed as he walked toward me.

"You can sit down, you know." He laughed quietly as I handed him his drink.

Our fingertips touched.

Sparks again.

"Well, I didn't know if you had a preference on the side of the bed. People can be really picky about their beds."

"You're right." He sat down on the bed and scooted to the side closest to the wall. He took a sip of his drink and patted the empty spot next to him.

I gulped and hoped the sound wasn't as noticeable out

loud as it was in my head. Those damn nerves were really trying me.

I slipped off my shoes and sat down next to him. He was on top of his comforter, so that left the whole guessing on what to do for that off the table. The remote was somewhere hidden next to him. He grabbed it and pressed play on the menu.

We talked a little between scenes. I asked him questions about the movie. Yes, I can be one of *those* people—people who won't just shut up and watch the movie. But I had a good excuse this time. I didn't want to watch the movie in silence. I wanted to talk to the man. I wanted to enjoy his company.

He got up a few times and refilled our drinks. Yes, a few times. *The Wolf of Wall Street* is a very long movie. Heat was forming in my limbs and in my stomach and in my . . . that whole 'whiskey makes me frisky' thing is real, people.

As the movie got close to ending, the talking turned to touching turned to kissing turned to us being all over each other. I wanted him. Bad.

That whole 'whiskey dick' is also a real thing.

We tried so many times to get it to work . . . but it wouldn't . . . or couldn't. He had a name for his dick. I can't really remember what it was, but for all intents and purposes, we'll say he called it Richard.

After the umpteenth attempt to shove it in my vagina, I rolled over, out of breath, and sighed in frustration.

"Richard doesn't want me," I pouted. Don't forget I'm more than three glasses of whiskey and ginger ale in, here. I was a whiny bitch, but I was a drunk whiny bitch. Blame it on the alcohol.

He rolled onto his back and let out his own sigh of frustration.

"Trust me. He does."

Phew . . . I wasn't the only one talking about his dick like there was another person in the room.

"Then why won't it work?"

"Come on, Cole. You know why. We drank too much. Give me a break. Please."

"Okay." I closed my eyes and tried to fall asleep.

I had just given up on getting any that night, when I felt pressure on my shoulder. Before I could think about if I had actually fallen asleep or not, I was pulled from the edge of the bed to the middle and flipped onto my back.

When my eyes finally adjusted and my heart started beating again, I realized OG was straddling me. I looked into his warm chocolate gaze, and then my eyes slowly traveled south. Richard was up. Like fully up and ready to show me what he was working with. As I looked at it longer, my eyes grew larger and I gulped. I didn't care if the sound was audible or not. I had never seen a Richard so large and so thick. I was kind of scared. Like, legit frightened. He was supposed to fit inside of me? I hadn't noticed the size before when I was sporting liquor-fogged glasses and he was a not-so-erect penis.

"You still want to?" OG asked, noticing my hesitation.

I gulped again. "Yes," I squeaked. I had just enough liquor left in me to give him the go ahead. To try. There was that liquid courage sinking in.

He laughed. "You sure?"

"Mmmmhmmm. Yeah."

"Okay."

He didn't say anything else as he ripped open a magnum condom wrapper. I watched him roll the rubber on and started second guessing myself. Just as he rolled it on the last inch, I stopped second guessing and began amping myself up. I was being my own hype man.

It's all right. You can do this. It'll fit. No worries, right? YOLO.

He's had sex before. Maybe I should have asked him if there's been any casualties.

Before I could officially freak out, Richard was working his way inside, trying to make himself at home. I thought the feeling you got the first time you had sex was one you only had to feel once. If I hadn't known I had had sex before this, I would have thought I was losing my virginity. That shit hurt like a motherfucker.

I bit my lip and closed my eyes and waited for that second feeling you get when you lose your virginity. The feeling that comes after the pain. The realization that this is sinful because nothing else in the world feels better.

It took a while, but my body adjusted, and the second wave came. We fucked all night. Richard was definitely worth waiting for.

* * *

NOT LONG AFTER my one night with The OG and Richard, I moved back to Athens. I started my new job and moved in with a friend from college who had a townhome with an available room.

Though we were miles apart, OG and I continued talking and struck up a 'relationship'. Y'all know what I mean. One of those things that's a relationship, but it's not. He's your boyfriend, not boyfriend. You're talking, but not together. Trying to 'see where things go' . . . yeah . . . it was one of those.

The first weekend OG came to visit me, I showed him around Athens. I took him to local restaurants. We went shooting at a gun range and drank a little . . . not at the same time, of course! It was great.

Though most of our visits were pretty good, there were a few times when he came out that weren't the best. Things slowly started to go downhill . . . you know how those things go.

One weekend he came to visit, my old roommate Cici from college was in town. She and her boyfriend were staying with me and so was OG. Cici had been on the dance team when we were in school and the dance team was putting on a show with the local high school, so she came down to help and provide support. Her boyfriend, Carter, was going to the show and she asked if OG and I would buy tickets and go as well. We worked it into our plans for that Saturday night.

Cici and Carter came in Friday night though, so we could go out and drink. When they showed up, Carter and OG really hit it off. They were both tall and laughed about the same things, so I guess that's why they got along so well.

When OG and I were upstairs in my room, getting ready, he came into the bathroom and stood behind me. I looked at him through the mirror and noticed a huge grin on his face.

"What's got you smiling so big?" I asked him.

"Your friends are cool." He wrapped his arms around my waist as I was putting my hair up.

"I think so." I couldn't help but grin back at his reflection.

"I had no clue you had black friends. I thought all of your friends were white." His grin got two times larger as he started cracking up.

I smirked and shook my head and finished getting ready.

That night must have been uneventful because I don't really remember what happened when we went out.

The next day before the show, the four of us went out to eat. I took them to this newer restaurant down the street from my house. I can't remember what it was called, but it was a burger joint. It was particularly amazing because their fries were awesome and they had what felt like hundreds of options for stuffed burgers. I'm not sure why at the time I thought that was just the best invention ever, but I loved those burgers. They were beyond cheesy. At least, the one I picked out was.

Anyway, we were sitting at a booth eating our food when some random guy walked in. He walked past us and when he did, Carter and OG turned to stare at one another. They gave each other a look and they both stood up and walked toward the back, following after the stranger.

Cici and I were beyond confused, but we shrugged our shoulders and kept tearing up our food. Not long after they had left, the boys returned. They sat down and resumed eating like nothing happened. The man who had come in ordered some food, and then he walked out after he got his bag.

I asked OG what happened. Carter started laughing and after he finished chewing the bite of food that was in his mouth, he looked up at me and Cici.

"We just bought some weed."

My eyes widened. I felt like one of those cartoon characters whose eyes pop out of their head.

"What?" I asked.

Cici put her burger down.

OG spoke up next. "Yeah, we just bought some weed. No big deal."

No big deal? At the time, I was very against weed. I won't get into the politics on that one. I don't have enough book for that. Weed just wasn't my thing. It's still not. But unlike I did then, now I don't judge, don't care—however you want to phrase it—when other people do it. To each his own. I'd just much prefer a vodka tonic or a whiskey ginger. But at the time, weed . . . to me . . . was a big deal.

"From who?" Cici asked. "That strange man who just came through here?"

"Yup," OG answered as he stuffed his mouth with fries.

"How did you even know he could sell you some weed?" I asked.

The two of them looked at one another and just started laughing.

"We just knew," OG answered. "He had a look about him."

Carter laughed. "Yeah," he agreed.

"Well, I hope y'all aren't expecting to smoke that at Cole's house," Cici said. She stared at the two of them as she popped the last bite of her burger into her mouth.

Cici knew how I felt about it and she knew that shit was not about to happen at my place. In college, she had smoked weed a few times at our small apartment. She was into it, but again, I wasn't. Though she smoked it occasionally, we were both on the same page about it being an outside activity, usually on the back porch.

They turned their attention from her to me. They looked like two little kids who were trying to get their mom to please let them have ice cream after dinner.

"Outside." I angrily finished the rest of my food.

When we got back to the house, Cici had to leave to get to the high school early. The guys and I were gonna walk over later. We had a couple of hours to kill and I wanted to take a nap before we left.

We had barely been in the house five minutes when OG kissed me on the cheek. "So . . ." Carter was looking at me with puppy dog eyes too.

"I told you—outside. Y'all can go on the back porch, and if the cops roll up, you can deal with it. Don't come back inside this house."

"Yes, ma'am."

The two of them went outside, and I headed upstairs for a nap.

* * *

THERE WAS another time OG came to Athens for a visit and we went downtown and got hammered. We bar hopped to a few places and got a taxi back home. Yes, there was a time before Uber and Lyft.

My roommate, Marsha, was home and was upstairs in her room. I didn't know if she was awake or asleep, but her TV was on, her door was shut, and the cat was in her room with her. As I locked the front door and reset the alarm behind us, OG lost it. And I'm not talking about hurling chunks all over the floor—though that would have really pissed me off. I mean, like full-on started going nuts.

He was slightly more intoxicated than I was, which still to this day, I do not know how it was possible. He had like an entire foot on me and drank fewer drinks than I did. Anyway, he mumbled some random stuff and crawled around on the floor. He started lifting couch cushions and pillows and then he crawled over to my feet.

I looked down at him and he stared back up at me with red eyes. "Where's Kitty?"

Kitty was what we called my roommate's cat.

I shrugged my shoulders. "Probably upstairs with Marsha." I moved my foot from underneath his hand. "Come on, let's get some water and go upstairs."

I turned to head into the kitchen.

"MARSHA."

I turned around quickly. OG wasn't in the living room anymore. I started toward the stairs.

"MARSHA. Where's Kitty?!"

He was crawling, unsuccessfully, up the stairs.

"Where's Kitty?! . . . MARSHA!"

"Will you shut up?" I whisper-yelled.

I tried to grab onto him, but I couldn't get a good hold on him.

"MARSHA. KITTY," he continued yelling.

"OG, stop," I said through clenched teeth.

Somehow, he made it to the top of the stairs. Just as he was about to knock on Marsha's door, I finally got a hold of his shirt. I grabbed him and pushed him across the tiny hall into my room.

The next morning when we woke up, he looked over at me, clearly hungover. "Your roommate is gonna be so mad."

She was.

He eventually apologized and Marsha and I laugh about it now, but it was not a fun night.

* * *

ANOTHER NIGHT IN ATHENS, another night of drinking. OG was visiting again and so were Cici and Carter. Another friend from college and her brother were also in town for the weekend. Cici and Carter and Tawny and her brother were all staying at a hotel. There wasn't enough room at my place and Carter had some allergy issues with Kitty the last time they'd stayed the night. We all decided to go out. Shocker.

Carter and Cici came and picked up me and OG and we met the other two at the hotel. We pregamed a little, took pictures, and then headed out to downtown. The hotel was close enough for us to walk. Afterward, the four staying at the hotel were going to walk back and OG and I were going to get a taxi back to my place.

All the bars in Athens closed at two in the morning. My house wasn't super close to downtown, so there was a trick to getting home at the end of the night. I told OG we would have to leave around 1:15 or 1:30 because if we waited until 2 a.m., we would never get a taxi. The drivers wouldn't go that far out and miss their chance at multiple opportunities with passengers who lived closer. They could get three rides in during the time it would take to get to my house and back. When the bars closed, it was their primetime.

When I explained this to OG at the beginning of the night, he understood. When 1:15 came around, he somehow didn't. When 1:30 hit, he was still confused. And when it was 1:45, he was straight up ignoring me.

At 2 a.m., I was livid. Our friends were walking back to their hotel and I was stuck trying to find us a ride home while dragging around a shit-faced OG. Cici told me to let her know when we made it home safely.

It was 3 a.m. when I realized we weren't getting a taxi back. OG was too drunk to walk the distance to my house. It would have taken us at least an hour. I reached in my purse and grabbed my phone. I called Cici and it didn't take many rings for her to answer.

"Hello?"

"Cici . . ."

"Did y'all make it home okay?"

"Nope."

"What do you mean?"

"There are no taxis left and nobody would take us home. I told OG we needed to leave early." I looked over at him angrily as he sat on the sidewalk.

"Oh no . . ."

"Are any of y'all sober enough to come pick us up and take us home? I have twenty dollars."

There was silence for just a nanosecond. I really did not want to walk home . . .

"Yeah. I can come get you, but I don't need your twenty."

It wasn't long before Cici's car pulled up. I tried to give her the money, but like she had said on the phone, she wouldn't take it. When we pulled up to my house, I thanked her profusely and stuck the twenty in her purse, which was sitting on the center console between her and Carter.

Once we made it up to my room, OG and I argued a little bit. During the time it had taken us to get home, he had sobered up a bit and I think he understood the trouble he had caused. I washed my face and took off my clothes and hopped into bed. I tried to get Richard up to have some fun and maybe salvage the night. It was the least he could do. However, OG refused me. He wouldn't give me what I wanted. That drunk, whiny bitch came out of me and we argued about that too.

* * *

ATHENS WASN'T the only place where things were sour for us. Not long after I had moved, I went back to Kennesaw to visit my friends and spend some time with OG.

The two of us rented a hotel room near the department store where I used to work. We invited a few of our coworkers from the store to come over and pregame with us in the room before we headed out for the night. After taking a few shots, we somehow got to the bar down the street.

Some time during the night, things started to go badly. OG and I got into a huge argument. I couldn't tell you what it was about, but I can tell you it was bad. We were shouting. Well, mostly I was shouting at him and he was laughing at me.

At some point, I ended up outside and barefoot, walking down the road. By myself. OG eventually caught up to me and asked what I was doing. He asked why I was being so crazy. We all know how asking a woman why she's acting crazy usually ends up. Not good.

OG got me back to the room, but instead of trying to make up with me, that man left me in the room by myself and went back to the bar. I wanted to go home, but OG told me 'we paid for the room, we're staying in it.' Seeing as how I couldn't go anywhere due to my intoxication, I was stuck.

I must have blacked out after he left me because apparently some shit happened that I don't remember.

OG told me I had engaged the security bar at the top of the door to the hotel room because when he tried to get back in after his night at the bar, he couldn't. He said he yelled and banged on the door for a long time before I finally "woke up" and "walked" over to the door and unlocked it. I guess I didn't bother to put any clothes on to let him in because when I opened the door, I was butt ass naked. So he says.

He told me that wouldn't normally be a problem, except one of our friends had come back with him to check on me. Part of me believed him because I do sleep naked, but it's not like he hadn't seen it before, so why did it matter? There was another part of me that didn't believe the story at all. Either way, I had no recollection of locking or unlocking the door.

However, it definitely must have happened because when I saw that friend again, he smiled and started laughing.

"What's so funny?" I asked him.

"Nice tits."

I couldn't help cracking up myself.

* * *

WHEN THINGS WERE GOOD, they were good. When they were bad, they were bad. The relationship or whatever it was between us was dwindling. A few times when we talked over the phone, he was distant and kept saying things like he 'was never going to be able to provide for me' and 'things weren't stable in [his] life right now'. Other times, we would laugh and cut up for hours.

One weekend, he was supposed to come visit me. We hadn't set up a plan exactly, but the idea had been discussed.

One day we were texting like normal and the next day, it was radio silence.

I bet you've been wondering throughout this whole episode, why I've been calling this man The OG. As far as I was concerned, he wasn't an Original Gangsta. I call him The OG because, in my life stories, he is The Original Ghost.

At the time, I don't think the term "ghosting" was a thing, but that's essentially what he did. One day he was in my life and then he just wasn't. He disappeared. I sent him multiple texts and phone calls, but I never heard back from him. He was gone.

* * *

A SHORT TIME LATER, I found myself working at that department store again doing loss prevention. OG didn't work there anymore, but most of my other friends from the store were still there. One of them, Jan, worked in the makeup department. She knew everything that had happened between OG and me and how things abruptly ended.

Jan called me on the office phone one day.

"OG is about to come in here."

"What?" I asked.

"Yeah, he just text me and asked if I was working. I told him yeah and he said he was shopping at the mall with his sister, so he's gonna stop by and say hey."

Jan had gone to high school with his sister, so they all knew each other relatively well, outside of having been coworkers.

"Are you serious?"

"As a heart attack."

"Well, I'm not about to come down there." I was over it at this point.

"Oh no, no. I wasn't saying come do that. I just wanted

you to know, so you wouldn't freak out if you saw him on the camera."

"Oh, okay, cool. Thanks."

Of course I turned the cameras for that department on the monitors. I watched him walk in and saw that huge, beautiful smile on his face. He looked good. He looked happy . . . without me.

I turned the cameras to something else and not long after, Jan called me back in the office.

"Did you see him?" she asked.

"Yeah. He looked good."

"Yeah, he's doing pretty good. I had to put him in his place though."

"What do you mean?" I asked.

"Well, I casually brought up your name."

"And?" I needed her to continue. My interest was piqued.

"He and his sister looked at each other and just started laughing. I asked them what was so funny, and his sister said, 'Man, that girl is crazy. She wouldn't leave my brother alone for the longest.' Then they started laughing again."

My heart slowly cracked open again as I listened.

"But then I crossed my arms and gave OG an evil look. 'Did you tell your sister what *you* did?' I asked him. And his sister, was like 'What are you talking about, Jan?' She looked over at her brother, wondering what I was about to bring up. 'Well, your brother just stopped talking to her. He was supposed to go see her and just stopped all communication with her. No text, no call, no explanation. Months of them talking and he just bailed and didn't let her know he was doing it.'"

"What happened next?" I asked.

"The smile wiped right off both of their faces and she smacked him hard as she could. Apparently when he was talking shit about you to his sister, he left out some details. Don't worry, I got your back, girl."

"Well, thanks. I really appreciate it."

I hung up the phone and shook my head.

This bitch . . . and Richard too.

* * *

So, there was a short five month period when I was in Athens starting that new job, you know. Yeah, well, I wasn't there long enough and I was too busy working in that short time frame to do any new dating. It all comprised of the craziness that was OG. And then I couldn't complete some required training in a timely manner, so I found my ass back at my mom's house and back working at that same department store. I will be forever grateful to them for letting me have my job back. However, I found myself 'dating' (let's use that term loosely) people in the store again. At least this time, I *managed* to move up the ranks. Eh, eh? See what I did there? No? Well, you'll get it when you see the title of the next episode. Enjoy.

EPISODE 7

THE MANAGER

*T*here was a guy once. Well, you've pretty much got the theme of this story by now—at least, I would hope—so of course there was . . . there was a plethora. I had to find some way to fit that word into my book. It's my favorite.

Anyway, where were we? Oh yeah! This guy. *This guy* was sexy. So very, very sexy. I remember him vividly and always will. If I could put an emoji into this part of the book, it'd be the thumbs up, the winky face, and the one with the hand making the "okay" sign. You know the one I'm talking about; the one where you make an "o" with your thumb and pointer finger and the rest of your fingers are sticking up?

Well, not that one! But look, you can put emojis into a book!

So, to begin again, this man was a hot piece of ass. He was a manager at the same department store where I worked with OG. I always thought he was hot, but he seemed a little standoffish. Plus, I was told he may have a girlfriend, and he was a manager. Granted he wasn't *my* manager, and with my position, we were *technically* on a level playing ground, but based on the other factors combined, I marked an X on his forehead. Uh uh. Off limits. Just eye candy. Beautiful, beautiful eye candy. And with the way he wore his pants, it was hard not to stare. I had never seen a man wear pants so tight before and actually pull it off. His thighs were amazingly muscular and you could see the outline of everything. Everything.

So, I figured out how to put an emoji in this text, but I think it's impossible for me to insert a GIF. Gosh, if I could insert GIFs into a book, I'd write an entire book just made completely of GIFs. If you know me, you know my obsession. Right here, would be the perfect place to put a GIF of someone wagging their eyebrows up and down. I'll repeat the sentence, so you can get a visual here.

His thighs were amazingly muscular and you could see

the outline of everything. Everything. *Insert eyebrow wagging GIF here.

I swear I wasn't being a creeper. We ALL noticed it. Trust me, I know because we ALL talked about it. However, the man pulled it off and I always say, if you got it, flaunt it.

It was months before anything happened. I was talking to OG, he had the X on his forehead, etc., etc. (*Etc.* is coming out of my mouth the same way James McAvoy's character in *Split* said it . . . well, one of the many characters he played in that movie. By the way, if you haven't seen *Split* and you value my opinion at all, you need see it. It's amazing. I'm not getting paid anything whatsoever to say that).

I'm not quite sure how it happened, or I don't remember, anyway, and those texts are long deleted off of my phone, but Manager and I started conversing. Somehow, he ended up being invited to the New Year's Eve party Biff and I were hosting at her house. It was intended to be low-key with just a few people, but shit got weird.

I really wish I could remember how our talking had started or what lead up to me inviting this man to Biff's house. I must have done some real good convincing because I do remember I was not entirely sure if Manager was attracted to me. I'm usually pretty positive (read: almost certain) when someone is feeling me, but I wasn't too sure about this one. He sent mixed signals and then there was the whole thing about him possibly having a girlfriend, but no one was really sure, and maybe he wasn't really into girls, and I have no clue how he ended up at the party, but he ended up at the party.

There was the revelation that he was really into Taylor Swift, which drunk Biff and drunk me also really loved. We all sang along to Taylor on the television, as true Swifties do, and took Jell-O shot after Jell-O shot.

Some other people showed up to party with us, and we all

had a blast, drinking dranks, dancing dances, and taking pictures of each other to post on our social media accounts. Manager was a little apprehensive of who else from work was going to show up, but after he realized it was just one guy—we'll call him Bob—he relaxed again.

Bob was a temporary holiday hire who had actually been my neighbor growing up. We didn't speak after I graduated from high school, but once he came to work at the store, we were just as cool as we had been before I left. He had a crush on Biff, so of course he was going to show up at the house. He was pretty chill, and Manager wasn't worried about him being there, so he continued to let loose.

As the night went on, Bob got drunker and drunker. Or is it more drunk and more drunk? I'm not sure, but dude got wasted. Shwasted. Like, white girl wasted. It was bad. He was trying so hard to talk to Biff, trying to get close to her, to be on her team during beer pong (which was actually liquor pong), and everything else. It wasn't working; Biff wasn't interested. But as drunk people tend to be, Bob was oblivious.

He continued drinking to maintain a certain level of liquid courage, but the party ended as soon as he barfed all over Biff's living room.

Yeeeeaaahhh . . .

Music stopped. TV turned off. Games abruptly ended. Cups were no longer lifted to lips for sips of the poison. All movement ceased to exist.

And then Biff went into a rage.

I don't remember exactly how things went, but I know Manager started cleaning up the vomit. I couldn't do it. I've gotten better as time has gone on when it comes to vomit, but at the time it was a big no. Nuh uh. No way. Don't even ask me. And the smell was putrid, so it definitely wasn't happening.

Somehow Bob managed to get himself cleaned up and changed. I still don't know where the clean clothes came from. It's one of the great mysteries in life.

As Manager was cleaning up the last of the puke, Bob made one of the biggest mistakes of his life. He attempted, yet again, to talk to Biff. *insert face in palm emoji

(again . . . not the right emoji, but you get the point).

She was not happy and literally almost kicked him out. Mind you, this was before ride sharing apps were a thing. No, I will not tell you how old I am. Just know I'm still in my twenties as I write this, so I'm still young.

Biff literally pushed Bob outside. I had to convince her that wasn't a good idea. He was drunk and a plethora of bad things could happen to him out in the wild in the middle of the night. (1. We did make it past the ball drop before this all happened; 2. I used plethora again—in the same episode!—so that kinda makes me a boss ass bitch.)

Biff simply looked at me and then past me at Bob standing outside, looking in.

"Come on, Biff, let him in. It's cold." (It was New Year's Eve, remember. Even in Georgia, it's cold as a bitch outside, especially when you have no jacket).

Without a word, she grabbed a pillow and throw blanket off the small couch in the walk-in area. She walked toward the front door, flung it open, and threw the shit outside before slamming the door shut. Then she looked at me again.

I tilted my head to the side. "Biff . . ."

"No!" was all she said.

"Manager cleaned it all up and Bob isn't gonna drink anymore. Just let him come inside to sleep."

She stared at me for a few minutes and then sighed heavily. "Fine, but he sleeps by the door, on the floor."

Now that I could work with.

"Okay."

I went and got Bob from outside and told him the rules. He immediately lay on the floor and fell right to sleep. No problems.

Nothing ends a party like barf flying everywhere. Most guests had gone, except for Biff's "friend" who was waiting for her in her room and one other person sitting on the couch.

I walked back into the kitchen, grabbed my drink off the counter, and headed into the living room. I plopped on the couch and let out a sigh.

Manager looked over at me and our eyes locked. We both grinned and laughed quietly at the situation.

"Well, that was disgusting," I finally said.

"Yeah . . . it should be all good tomorrow. At least it doesn't smell anymore."

"Very true. And all thanks to you for cleaning it up." I raised my glass to him and took a sip of the vodka in my hand.

"Yeah. It's no big deal. And I probably wouldn't be sitting on that couch if I was you."

I jumped up immediately. "Why?"

"There was a little bit of throw up on the cushions." He

laughed at the look of horror on my face.

I turned around and swiped at my ass. "Did I get any on me?"

"No. You look fine."

We stared at one another. I walked over and joined him on the clean couch.

I couldn't tell you how it happened. I can't say whether it was the booze, the tight pants, the sexy face, or the fact that he cleaned up vomit without hesitation and did a damn good job at it too, but the next thing I knew, my drink was on the coffee table, my pants were at my ankles, and Manager was on top of me and inside of me.

The way he filled me up definitely proved that the outline in his pants was not a deception. I won't forget the way he felt or the look on his face as he thrusted in and out of me. However, there is one thing that always springs to my mind whenever I happen to think of Manager . . .

"You made me come."

That's what he said as his nut filled the condom around his dick. That's what he said as his face twisted in pleasure and . . . confusion?

Manager seemed completely and utterly bewildered at the fact that I had made him come. I am still, to this day, perplexed by the statement he made right before he pulled out of me.

I didn't say a word. My eyes darted back and forth as I looked for anyone, anything that may have heard what I just heard. I kept myself from cracking up.

"You made me come?"

Uuuuh . . . isn't that the point?

Manager pulled up his pants and I pulled up mine. I grabbed my drink from the table and he plopped down on the couch. The other couch. The couch that supposedly had vomit on it.

EPISODE 8

✣

THE BACON

*L*et's talk about the night I ate too much bacon and got bacon drunk. It's seriously a thing! And getting bacon drunk is the best thing ever, but the things that happen when you're bacon drunk . . . not so much.

There was this guy who had a little crush on me. This guy's friend/roommate was dating Biff. I forget how they met, but they were a thing for a little while. Biff begged me to go with her to their house. I had met the one with a crush on me before—he's Bacon, which is actually kind of confusing because I really did eat too much literal bacon. So if I'm talking about the food, the word won't be capitalized, while the man will get the luxury of his name for this book being a proper noun: Bacon.

Anyway, I had met him before and could tell he was into me, but he wasn't really my type. I couldn't tell you what exactly my type was, but I knew he wasn't it. I wasn't really looking forward to going over, especially knowing I'd have to take one for the team so Biff could spend time with the other guy. I'll call him Scott. Don't ask me why . . . it's just the first name that popped into my head.

We made it over to Scott and Bacon's house and we chilled for a little bit. There was some event going on. I can't remember if it was a big football game or what, but something was going on that was aired on TV and that required cooking out and chilling. After hanging out for a bit at the house, we went to the mall. When we got back, Bacon started grilling some food. It was mostly staples: hot dogs, hamburgers, some chicken, plus there were chips and other side items in the kitchen. But there was one food he cooked that I won't ever forget: bacon wrapped asparagus.

Now, I love asparagus, so he could have just thrown some of that on the grill and I would have been a happy girl. However, he put bacon on them. Baaaaaacon (I know that was capitalized, but bear with me, I was talking about the food).

Pretty much the entire time we were over at the house, I was ready to go home. I had texted The Manager at some point while I was in the restroom and asked him to come pick me up, but he would not. Something about he was with his friends or was doing something completely expected and he was too stunned to do anything else. Yes. That was a jab.

I was stuck. Biff was boo'd up with Scott and I was trying to keep myself far on the opposite end of the couch from Bacon. I shrugged my shoulders and said, 'fuck it.' No, not fuck it, like I was gonna scooch down and join Bacon on the right side of the couch. 'Fuck it' as in, I needed a fucking drink. Not having fun? Just add liquor.

I made myself a drink and started to loosen up a little bit. Bacon seemed less pushy and less unattractive and less annoying the more alcohol I consumed, but I didn't want to get too sloshed. Not at this house. I knew what Bacon was after and he wasn't getting it from me.

After fixing my third drink, I told myself no more. I was

babysitting the drink in my hand when I got a whiff of bacon. My mouth immediately started watering and I started looking around to discover the source of the heavenly smell. That's when I noticed Bacon bringing over a tray of bacon-wrapped asparagus.

He put it on the table for all of us to share and plopped back down on the couch. I put my drink down and snatched one off the tray. I didn't care that my fingers burned from the heat. I put that thing in my mouth, bit down, and started chewing. It was amazing. My mouth is literally watering right now as I'm writing this piece. I looked over at Bacon and stared at him in awe. I grabbed another piece and finished it just as quickly.

I guess Bacon realized how happy his food had made me. He had a huge grin on his face and got up quickly to go make another batch. I finished my drink while I waited and it didn't take long for him to bring out another tray of the treat conjured up by the gods. Scott, Biff, and I had started playing a card game when Bacon came in with the food.

"Here. I made you another drink. I saw you finished your other one," he said to me as he handed me something in a plastic cup.

"What is it?" I asked.

"Same as before."

I grabbed the cup, took a sip and put it on the table. Who really cared about the drink when there was more bacon to be eaten?

Just like the first tray, the second tray was gone almost instantaneously. Bacon got up to cook some more.

"There's no more bacon," he hollered from the kitchen.

I gasped. He just spoke blasphemy. What were we going to do?

"We can go to the store," Scott spoke up.

"Who's gonna drive?" Biff asked.

Bacon came back in the living room from the kitchen. "I can drive. I've only had a beer."

I stood up expeditiously. "Well then. Let's go. The bacon's waiting for us." I gathered my purse and jacket and put on my shoes. I was on a mission.

We all climbed in the car and made it to the store in one piece. Bacon tried to hold my hand, but I wasn't feeling it. I couldn't risk giving his magical bacon hands any bad juju. I needed more bacon wrapped asparagus perfection.

After we got back to their place, Scott and Biff found their places back on the couch. I sat down on the floor and Bacon found his spot preparing the food. He made the entire pack of bacon this time. Good boy.

We ate the remaining snackums and I'm not sure what happened between the last bite of food I had and when I woke up, but something had definitely transpired.

The last I remembered, I was in the living room sucking bacon grease off my fingers. When I woke up, I was in the bedroom, and Bacon was licking the juice between my legs.

Oh. Hell. No.

I hurriedly moved up the bed and hopped out of it.

"Wait. What happened? Did I do something wrong?" he asked as I found my clothes scattered around the room.

"Nope," was all I said.

"What?"

"Nope. Nope. Uh uh."

I got dressed and walked out of Bacon's room. I knocked on Scott's door and told Biff we had to go. After a few minutes, she came out and found me sitting on the couch. Alone.

"We gotta go." I stood up and headed for the door.

Biff and I knew each other well enough that she recognized she shouldn't ask any questions. Not yet anyway. She said bye to Scott and we walked to her car.

"What happened, Cole?"

"Who knew bacon could drug you?"

EPISODE 9

❧

THE RAPPER

*I*t all started with a dating app . . .

    I joined Plenty of Fish a few months after I became single. I was ready to mingle. *Bet you haven't heard that one before. This was before Tinder was a thing. I promise you, I'm not that old.*

After speaking with a few guys on POF, I encountered The Rapper. He was attractive and had a great smile. His skin was dark chocolatey and smooth, and he was so sweet. We talked on the phone several times. He made me laugh and I got those little butterflies in my stomach every time his name popped up on my phone.

One day, he finally asked if he could take me on a date and meet me in person. I told him I would love that, and we planned to go to a restaurant that was in between both of our homes. He had an apartment in Austell, and I was living in Dallas. And by Dallas, I mean Georgia.

My sister and her boyfriend at the time insisted on driving me. They said they would be close by in case anything happened and that way I could have a drink or two to loosen me up if things were awkward.

Rapper and I agreed on a time, and after taking hours to put on the perfect outfit and get my makeup just right, I hopped in my sister's car. It took us about twenty minutes to get there and when we arrived, I sent Rapper a text to let him know I was there. I didn't know what kind of car he drove, so I couldn't point him out.

He texted back not too long after and said he was running late. I can't remember exactly what the reason was for his tardiness because something more awful happened once we got inside.

Rapper finally showed up after I waited for at least half an hour. He was even more attractive in person. I've got a thing for teeth and his were perfect. They were straight and pearly white and thinking about his smile still gets me. *You can add a word to the end of that sentence if you want to. Insert shoulder shrug emoji.* I was a very happy girl.

We walked inside and were seated at a booth. The date itself went well. We laughed and had a lot to talk about. It was my first time meeting him, but there wasn't an awkward moment at all—that is, until we finished eating. *That awful thing I mentioned? That thing worse than making me wait for half an hour? It's about to happen.*

"I want to come sit next to you," he said with that gorgeous grin plastered on his face.

"Oh, no." I laughed.

"What you mean, 'oh no'?"

"I can't stand when people sit on the same side in a booth."

"Really?" he asked. "Why?"

I shrugged my shoulders. "I don't know. I just think it's weird. Every time I see people do it, it just creeps me out."

Rapper simply stared at me from across the booth where he belonged, still smiling.

"Besides," I continued, "I can't look at you while we talk if you're sitting next to me."

"Oh, come on. Let me come over there."

We were both smiling really hard at this point, just having a staring contest. I don't know if he thought I was joking or not, but Rapper got up and walked over to my side of the booth. And then he sat down. The next thirty minutes of the date were awkward as hell and I definitely ordered that second drink. It was the longest thirty minutes of my life.

* * *

THE SECOND TIME I hung out with Rapper was a few days later at Biff's house. She and her roommates were throwing some kind of house party. She said it was cool to invite him. Some of our other mutual friends came, along with her roommates' friends, and my sister and her boyfriend.

When Rapper got drunk, I found something out about him I hadn't known before. He was an aspiring musician . . . a rapper. He started showing off all his music to my friends and it sounded pretty good. Everyone seemed to like his stuff and him, so I thought maybe my dating woes would soon be over.

At some point during the party, Rapper pushed me up against a wall where no one else was around. We shared our first kiss and it was just as amazing and thrilling as I had imagined it would be all of those times I had pictured it in my head.

We slept on the couch, fully clothed—no funny business —and I drove him home the next morning before dropping my sister and her boyfriend off. At one point during that drive, I may have taken a curve too fast and caused everyone to hold on for dear life. It's funny now how that one incident was a premonition of what was to come in this relationshit: Move too fast and you might get killed.

* * *

THE RAPPER LIVED in a one-bedroom apartment in Austell. He let one of his brothers live with him, so the brother slept on the couch. The Rapper worked from home and I worked in retail, so for the most part, our schedules gelled. Sometimes when I got off work, I would go over to his place and stay the night and other times, I would stay the night and then go straight to work from there.

We hung out, drank draanks, watched TV and movies, went shopping . . . basically did a lot of things together. Yes, we eventually had sex, but I won't get into too much detail about it because this isn't that type of book. However, I will say it was because of Rapper that I was introduced to analingus and shmegma. That being said, it was very good, but sometimes it stunk. Pun very much intended.

I thought we were getting along great. We did things for each other and there were good vibes between us. We even decided on a couples costume for Halloween. Then one weekend Rapper decided he wanted to go out. Without me. That's when I realized we never had actually gone out together. Sure, we had gone out to grab some food a couple of times. And by that, I literally mean two times: our first date and the one time we went to Applebee's. We had never gone out and done anything. There were no other dates. We didn't go bowling, hiking, clubbing, or to a bar.

I asked if I could go with him and he told me no. I was upset. We texted that night while he was out, but the messages just stopped coming. It was like OG all over again. I tried for almost a week to get a response out of him. The last thing he texted me was completely normal, so when it suddenly ceased, I kind of got worried about what had happened to him that night.

Over the next few days, I figured Rapper was just done with me and was probably okay. I had left some food over at his house so, I text him one last time and told him I needed to come get some of my things that were at his house. Shockingly, I got a response and he said I could come over to grab my stuff.

When I got there, Rapper was in the middle of working. I can't remember the company he worked for or what exactly it was that he did, but I know he answered the phone and provided some sort of computer support. If he wasn't on the phone, he wasn't doing anything, just waiting for the next call.

When I first got there, Rapper was in the middle of assisting someone over the phone. I came in and sat on his floor. Normally, I would have climbed into his bed, but I didn't figure it was appropriate anymore. He finished his call and hung up.

"What did you need, Cole?"

I just stared at him, waiting for him to look at me.

"You can just get it and go." He still wouldn't look at me.

I felt tears building. "What did I do?" I asked.

"Nothing."

"So why are you doing this?"

"We just aren't a good fit, Cole."

"How is that? We were literally fine a few days ago and then you just ignored me."

"Look," he started, "I'm just feeling a certain type of way."

"What is that?" I asked.

He finally looked over at me. "We just don't work. You're you and I don't like it anymore. And I feel like you're using me for my apartment."

The tears evaporated. Just like that. "Excuse me?"

He put himself on break and took off his headset, sitting up to get a better look at me. "You don't like being at your mom's house and here, you have a place to stay."

"You seriously think I like you for your apartment?" *What in the actual fuck?*

"Yeah and beyond that, you're too much."

This is where I should probably share with you all that I suffer from depression and anxiety. I'm not talking about the depression and anxiety that we all suffer through at some point during our lives. I'm talking about the kind that gets diagnosed by a doctor and you're prescribed medication for. I knew about the anxiety up to this point, but I wasn't aware about the depression until this event right here.

I don't want to get too deep into it because this is not a therapy session, but I was suffering. Majorly. I didn't feel good about myself. I didn't value myself. I was beyond sad. There's no way to simply put it into words. I can't describe how I was feeling because a part of me was trying to ignore the bad thoughts I was having.

There's a chemical imbalance at play with the whole depression thing and when Rapper said I'm just me *negatively* and I'm too much, I lost it. I don't know why I let his words have so much power over me, but they did. I almost killed myself that day after I left his house, but something steered my car back in the right lane and I made it home just in time to collapse on the floor and call my mother to get the help I needed.

Maybe that was the reason things turned out the way they did with Rapper. Maybe he was put in my life to push me so close to the edge to realize that I needed help.

I never heard from or about Rapper again. Guess the whole music thing didn't pan out.

EPISODE 10

THE DOCTOR

*D**ear Journal,***

Right now, as I'm writing this story, it's Halloween time. Though, I can hardly tell here in Georgia. It's still hot as balls and the leaves are barely falling off the trees. Anyhoo, it's the middle of October and my second favorite holiday is quickly approaching.

I'm not quite sure what I'm going to do for All Hallow's Eve this year, but nothing will ever compare to the Halloween I had a few years ago . . . 2014, maybe? That sounds about right. It was during the time I was living back at my mom's house after college before what I thought would be my dream job could become an actual thing. Though I was living with my mom, I practically also lived with my best friend, Biff, and her roommates. At least I did on the weekends.

Biff told me about this party going on at a fancy hotel in Atlanta and, of course, I was like yaaaaasssss, let's go! Halloween? Drinks? Party? Is that even a real question? Things had just ended with the guy who wanted to be a musical artist and I'd loved his apartment a little too much and I was ready to get drunk and enjoy a night of just having fun. The two of us were supposed to do a couple's costume. Like, who seriously talks to someone about wearing a couple's costume for Halloween one minute and then is like, nah, never mind, in the next? I don't get it, but then again, here I am writing about being single. I digress.

After a couple of weeks of thinking and shopping in a couple of stores, I finally decided on a slutty school girl costume. I wasn't going to be just any slutty school girl. Oh no, no, no. I was going to be a slutty school girl who had died. A dead slutty school girl. I concocted an entire backstory for my character, just in case somebody asked. And because, as you know, I write things.

No one asked.

So, I'll tell you.

Nicole was a girl who was in school. She had to wear a uniform to school. The uniform was a short pink plaid skirt and a tucked in white blouse. Nicole's breasts were large, so she took it upon herself to pop off the top two buttons so her lady friends could breathe.

Nicole was a little bit of a slut. She loved to have sex and suck cock (personally, I don't see anything wrong with that). One day, while she was slurping on some penis, she died. The penis was so large, her eyes watered the entire time it was slamming the back of her throat, which caused mascara to run down her face. She forgot to put on waterproof that day.

While she was sucking on the large shaft, the girlfriend of the owner of the thing came into the room. The girlfriend was so mad that Nicole was sucking her boyfriend's dick, she strangled her to death. And she never even got to wipe the mascara off her cheeks.

The End.

Okay, back to my story now.

So, I was the dead slutty school girl, Nicole, and Biff was the

Mad Hatter, but of course, dead. I'll skip through all the boring stuff of us getting there.

We got there and it was amazing. There were so many awesome costumes and so many drinks and a plethora of hot, hot men—from what I could see anyway, since they were in costume. It was like a dream come true.

Of course, we had pregamed at the house already and I was definitely a little toasted. One of my favorite vodka companies used to make this 100-proof vodka that tasted like root beer. Like, legitimately tasted like root beer. It didn't need a mixer and it was 100 proof. Dangerous stuff. I wonder if that's why they stopped making it?

Actually, that reminds me of this one time I was at a certain restaurant in Athens known for their large margaritas. For the longest time, they used to make Everclear margaritas (I could write an entirely different book on the adventures I have had with Everclear). For whatever reason, it was just never a good time to order one—I had to study, or I was driving, or I had had enough Everclear to last me a lifetime, etc.

One day, I was finally at the point where it was a go and I worked up the courage to finally ask for an Everclear margarita. I walked up to the bar and ordered one from the bartender with confidence. He looked at me and smirked and then said, "Oh girl, we don't make those anymore."

I was shocked. I couldn't believe the words coming out of his mouth. So, I opened my mouth. "Say what now?" I asked.

"Yeah, we had to stop making them. Too many people were getting sick."

Anyway, maybe that's why they stopped making the 100 proof root beer vodka. Just like the night I couldn't get my Everclear margarita, this makes me sad.

Anyway, for the second time, there was 100 proof root beer vodka in this story. And I drank a lot of it. It's possible the hot men weren't that hot, but in my mind's eye, they totally were.

One of the men who approached me was dressed in a doctor's costume. If I'm remembering correctly, he was pretty attractive, but the memory's vague. I can say with confidence that that night I thought he was sexy. He may have told me what his name was, but for as long as I can remember, I've always called him The Doctor. And that's not just me trying to protect someone's identity; I literally don't know his real name and don't think I ever have. Oh well.

"Wow, what are you supposed to be?" I asked him.

"A doctor," he answered in a sex kitten voice.

Is it supposed to be a sex kitten if it's a guy? I have no idea, but his voice was definitely sexier when he answered that question than it was for the rest of the night.

"Are you trying to come and see if I need any help?"

"Yes. That's what all good doctors do."

"Well, I'm dead. So, I don't need any help. Thank you."

It was a joke, Journal. A literal joke. I thought it was hilarious, but it stumped him. Or he didn't think it was very funny because he didn't laugh. But he did stick around and bought me shots. Must have been the boobs.

After hanging around with this guy for quite a while that night, there was one point where he disappeared. Either he actually disappeared or I just think he did because I'm recounting this story after years have passed by. But I do remember standing by this couch with my friends. It must have been some special couch because there were ropes around it. VIP, I'm guessing. Somehow, I managed to find myself underneath the ropes and sitting on the couch taking shots of very expensive vodka. Definitely not the root beer flavored shit I was taking back earlier in the night.

I had been on the couch for a while, leaned up against some other Halloween-costumed man, talking to him about who knows what, when The Doctor leaned over my shoulder and whispered into my ear.

"I see you found a new friend for the night. Someone else feeding you vodka."

I don't know why, at the time, this didn't offend me or make me angry. Or why I didn't just brush him off or ignore him or do anything other than what I did next.

I tilted my head back and saw The Doctor, upside down, staring at me. I cheesed super hard and replied with something along the lines of 'no, of course not'. I got up from the couch and rejoined him on the other side of the ropes.

Why did I leave the VIP and the fancy vodka behind me? I have no idea. I'm shaking my head as I'm writing this. I'm older and wiser and can afford fancy vodka for myself at this point, but I was younger, more naive, and most certainly could not afford fancy vodka, so what was I thinking?

I can guess it was because I was horny, and this guy must have been more attractive than the man on the couch. And what did I tell you at the very beginning of this thing? I was going through the phase. I couldn't help it. It wasn't my fault.

Somehow, Biff and I ended up at The Doctor's house, along with him and his roommates who had also been at the party. Biff had already arranged for them to give us a ride back to her house, so I had a couple of hours to do whatever it is I needed to do.

Though a lot of people are going to end up reading this, it's kind of like a private journal and I really hope the whole 'your parents shouldn't read your diary' thing applies here. Not only do I not want them reading about all the junk I hopped on, but I also really don't want a lecture about how reckless I was. Going to a stranger's house and being too drunk to get myself out of there if I needed to? Major red flags. Trust me. I know, Dad. I was being reckless. I've already yelled at myself plenty.

Back to the story.

So, I had a couple of hours. Who needs hours to get it done? If it takes hours, there might be a problem.

I am by no means a medical professional, so please do not take my word on that. And if you just can and want it to last for hours, well bravo to you. Seriously, bravo. I just wouldn't have the energy.

Anyhoo . . . I only needed a few minutes, I was sure.

The Doctor and I headed back to his bedroom. I remember it being a beautiful house and his room was spacious. Definitely not what I was used to, coming from four years of student housing.

I don't remember everything that lead up to what happened next, but y'all . . . I saw one for the very first time in my life. And I haven't seen one since.

It was right in my face.

A micropenis.

No, I did not misspell microphone in an attempt to describe what a honker The Doctor had.

It was a micropenis. Not too far away from my lips.

What am I supposed to do with that? I thought.

I smirked up at him and some weird, breathy choke sound came out of my throat.

I guess The Doctor thought that sound meant I was turned on because he grinned broadly and pushed me back on the mattress.

You know how they say it's not the size of the pencil, but how it writes? There is some truth to that, I guess. It wasn't quite as bad as I thought it would be. But it definitely was not . . . good. I'll give the guy some leeway though; I was drunk. Like, cheap 100 proof vodka mixed with expensive vodka drunk. There is such a thing as amazing, mind-blowing, drunk sex, but you've got to be a certain kind of drunk and I wasn't that.

Afterward, we lay in the bed, both on our backs, and stared up at the ceiling. My lips were pressed tight together and I was definitely ready to get out of there, but I wasn't quite sure how I was going to make my escape.

Remember earlier when he scolded me for talking to another man? I was sure he was gonna get all pissy if I suggested leaving him alone in his room after he had given me the d (I lowercased that for a reason).

I thought on it for a few minutes and then I told myself I had to go. I leaned over and kissed him on the cheek and said, "Boy, I wish we could go again, but I've really gotta go. It was really something." I kept a big smile on my face as I started searching around for my costume.

As I got dressed, I noticed a weird look on this kid's face. It almost looked as if he was upset I was leaving. I internally shrugged my shoulders and continued putting on my clothes.

I walked down the hallway and knocked on the door to the room I believed Biff to be in. She answered right away and I told her I was ready to go. I heard some talking on the other side of the door and she said the roommate she was with was going to take us home. I told her I would meet her in the living room.

I quickly walked back to The Doctor's room to grab the rest of my things. I asked him if he was riding with us and he looked at me like I just asked him the craziest question he'd ever been asked.

"Nah. I'm gonna just stay here."

I shrugged my shoulders outwardly this time and said, "Okay. Well, it was fun," as I walked back out the door to meet Biff and the roommate.

The whole car ride back was a little awkward, but I ignored it. I was drunk, happy, and though it was little, I'd just gotten some penis, so I wasn't complaining. Life was good.

The next day, Biff texted me and told me the roommate had been texting her and said The Doctor told him I was clingy.

What. In. The. Actual. Fuck? Clingy? Me? Clingy?

I started thinking and thinking and rethinking about what had transpired the night before. I was approached by him. I had moved on to the VIP section and then got pulled away by him. I was asked to go back to his place. I fucked a micropenis! A micropenis. I sat there and thought about how to politely leave his house. Leave, y'all. Leave. Not stay. Staying would be clingy, but I left!

What. In. The. Actual. Fuck?

I think this man mistook my politeness for being clingy. Calling me clingy? That doctor had terrible bedside manner. Needless to *say, I did not see that man again. Remember when I said I had only ever seen a micropenis once? I wasn't lying.*

On to the next one.

Again.

Forever yours whether you like it or not because I'm still single,

S

EPISODE 11

THE HOT MESS EXPRESS

*T*his guy . . . I never had so much fun in my life and yet, it just didn't work out.

Hot Mess was a manager at the large department store where I worked. Yes, the same one where The Manager worked and where OG worked. I promise you, it was just those three and I was involved with them at completely separate times. In fact, Hot Mess and I happened the second time I worked at the store while the other two were the first . . . I think.

Anyway, Hot Mess was pretty hot. Think surfer guy hot. He was Hispanic white with blonde hair and a goofy grin. He had tats on his forearm, and he was average build, but the man worked out constantly, so he was super toned underneath the button up shirts and dress slacks. He used to say the dumbest things and he would crack me up!

The first time I worked with Hot Mess, he was in a relationship. He had been with the woman for a long time and she had kids, so I figured they were serious. As a result, he was in the no-go zone. Couldn't do it.

When I went to work at the store the second time, Hot

Mess was no longer with the woman and he started looking ten times better than he had before. He used to come into my office and we'd crack jokes and have a good time.

One weekend we went out after work and had a great time. We drank and drank and did karaoke. Yes, I know I put drank twice in that sentence, but we did enough of it that it warranted repeating. He was a manager and I had a "higher up" position, but we both spent more than we should have when we went to this one bar with our coworkers.

It was a weekly thing. The guy who ran karaoke started recognizing us and eventually knew us by name. There was one time I was heading out the door and the karaoke man called me out on the microphone.

"Hey, Cole!"

I turned around while holding the door open and looked at him.

"I've gotta play your song before you leave!"

I stared at him longer and shut the door, returning to the table as soon as the beat dropped. I mean, it's a song about not fucking with someone anymore. Ahem . . . totally my life the past however many years. I couldn't leave. I had to stay and rap along with my peeps.

Thank you, Big Sean.

I tried to karaoke that song on stage once, and after a couple of drinks, I probably sounded like a professional rapper.

Like I said, we were there a lot.

One night, Hot Mess and I were at this bar with our friends. At this point, we were pretty much an item. There was no official title, so it was like every other thing I had going on after B, but we were a thing, nonetheless. Both of us wanted to get trashed that night, so we got a hotel room within walking distance of the bar.

After saying our goodbyes to our friends, we started

walking to the hotel. We were about halfway there when I realized how bad I had to pee. Really, I should have peed at the bar, but I thought I could hold it. The hotel wasn't that far, and I definitely preferred to piss in a reasonably clean hotel room versus the bar bathroom.

Meanwhile, I didn't focus on my bladder for the second half of the walk and we made it there pretty quickly. We got up to the door and Hot Mess started to pull on the handles.

"Madame," he said dramatically as he bent at the waist to attempt to hold the door open for me. It would have been cute, except for the fact the doors didn't budge.

I gasped. "What?"

The door was locked. Luckily, a few seconds later, somebody was coming out and let me and Hot Mess inside.

I practically ran inside toward the front desk, so we could check in and so I could tell them the front doors were locked. There was no one there. I was in shock. How were we supposed to check in? I had to pee. I needed to get up to the room. NOW.

"Where's the people?" he slurred.

"I don't know, Hot Mess, but I've really got to pee." I bounced around looking for a bathroom.

There wasn't one. What hotel doesn't have a bathroom in the lobby? I looked at the reservation on my phone to make sure I didn't miss reading a mandatory check-in time. Don't worry, I know what you're thinking. I booked the room online, but he gave me cash to cover the cost. Eeeeooowwww (said like Cardi B). I know that was bothering you.

Anyway, there wasn't a check-in time, and there wasn't a person. And there wasn't a bathroom. I called a number I found. I'm not sure what it connected me to, to be honest, but whoever I spoke to told me someone would be up or down shortly.

I waited shortly, but shortly sure did feel like longly because I couldn't hold it anymore.

"Hot Mess, I really gotta go." I started looking around frantically. "I'm gonna pee outside."

"What?" he asked, laughing.

"There were some bushes out front. I can't hold it anymore. I'm going. Just hold the door open for me, so I can get back in."

"Okay." Somehow, he managed to stumble over the simple word.

Hot Mess followed me to the front door and left it cracked open as I crawled my way to a spot in the bushes. There were some trees around, so I felt pretty safely hidden. I pulled my pants down and squatted. The stream started coming and I never felt something so wonderful and relieving in my life. Then I realized that, of course, my pee wasn't coming out straight like it would if I had a penis. It was traveling down my leg and all over my pants, but I couldn't stop. I had to pee so bad that I literally could not stop the urine from flowing.

I willed it to stop. I was halfway done—the rest could wait until we got up to our room. Nope, wasn't happening. And to make matters worse, I heard a car pull into the lot right next to where I was standing. I wouldn't have given two shits at that point—I was peeing all over myself—but when I looked over, I noticed a light bar on top of that shiny police car. I fell backwards in shock and landed on my ass in a pile of pee-soaked bushes. Somehow falling had hidden me from the cop because he or she kept driving and pulled out.

As I was lying on my back, all I heard was Hot Mess cracking the fuck up. He was laughing so hard, I was afraid he was about to lose all the air in his lungs.

"Are they gone for real?" I hollered up at him.

"Yes!" He continued laughing.

I somehow managed to stand up, pull my pants up, and walk back over to Hot Mess, who could barely hold the door open he was laughing so hard.

"I peed all over myself," I stated frankly as I walked past him into the lobby.

"I'm gonna call you P.P. Like piss pants and because like pee pee." He was cracking up again.

That was the kind of shit we got into.

Pun not intended, but that sure was punny.

* * *

THERE WAS another guy who hung out with me and Hot Mess pretty frequently—Nix. The three of us, along with Biff, would go out quite a bit. If we weren't at the karaoke bar, we were on Edgewood in Atlanta.

I'm not really sure who Nix was into. I don't know if he just wanted some sort of attention. There was one night he and Biff started to hook up, but she had to stop that real quick. She told me the next day that he was eating her out and he bit her. Down there. Hard. On purpose.

I mean people are into some different shit and no judgement, but that is a no-no for me and it obviously was a no-no for Biff.

Besides that, Nix seemed pretty cool. He was a little weird, but aren't we all? He was friendly and liked to have a good time and he was good friends with Hot Mess, so I was down to hang out with him.

There was one night just the three of us went out—Hot Mess, Nix, and me. I can't remember where we went; I think to just some beer bar. I wasn't really into beer at that time, so I didn't have much to drink that night. Afterward, we went back to Nix's place to crash. He had a one bedroom, so I fully expected Hot Mess and I were going to sleep in the living room.

We got there and Nix and Hot Mess started going toward Nix's room. I followed, hand in hand with Hot Mess. We all chilled for a bit, just talking about nonsense and bullshit. Nix had poured us some more drinks and we were hanging. After a while, though, things started to get a little weird.

Nix started rubbing all up on Hot Mess's leg. Hot Mess was clearly drunk and was just laughing and letting it happen. My eyes bugged out of my head. I had no clue what was going on.

"Have you ever been with two dudes?" Nix asked.

"Uh . . ." I couldn't get any words to form and spill out of my mouth.

I mean, it might have been really hot if Hot Mess hadn't been drunkenly laughing like he was when I peed my pants, or if I had been even remotely attracted to Nix. Put those two things together and it was less than hot. I wasn't feeling anything but awkward.

Nix leaned in and brushed his nose against Hot Mess's neck. "Well?" he asked.

"Nope," I responded.

"Are you interested?" He kept caressing Hot Mess's legs and arms.

Hot Mess looked like he had no clue what was really going on, but then he leaned in and the two of them started kissing. But not like full on, hot, sexy kissing. I mean like Eskimo kisses. They were rubbing their noses together.

"Uh . . ." was all I could muster again.

"Do you want to join, Cole?" Nix asked.

"Yeah, Cole. Come join our cuddling. Let's all cuddle," Hot Mess added.

"I don't think so. I'm just gonna go lay on the couch."

I started to get up to go. When Hot Mess stood to follow me, Nix lost his shit. He pitched a fit. A five-year-old fit. He stomped around and pouted and crossed his arms.

"Just forget it. *I'll* sleep in the living room."

"What?" I asked. "No. Come on. It's your house. You can sleep in the bed. I'll go in the living room." I was not about to speak for Hot Mess. I had no clue what he wanted to do.

"No! Y'all have a good night cuddling each other." And he stomped out of the room.

* * *

I MEAN SERIOUSLY, Hot Mess was a hoot. I called him Hot Mess because honestly, I couldn't think of anything better to call him. We had a blast and together, we were definitely aboard the Hot Mess Express.

In the end, we didn't work out. I don't know, I guess we just had too much fun together. Is there such a thing? I think there must be, since we never really got serious . . . about anything. The train abruptly stopped when it did and I was upset. We argued in that same parking lot OG and I had argued in that night I'd ended up butt naked in front of him and one of my friends. One of the girls who was there even called it deja vu.

"This is just like when you were arguing with OG."

After that, it was over. It needed to be.

I occasionally watch his Snapchats and reminisce on the good ole days. Except for when I see him post videos of him and his current girlfriend riding bikes—she can have that. Bike riding was the first date Hot Mess and I went on. I hadn't ridden a bike in years. I didn't forget how to ride it and it was fun, but I couldn't get out of the bed the next morning and when I finally forced myself out, I had to crawl up the stairs. Seriously. His girlfriend can have the bike rides. And Hot Mess.

PP out!

EPISODE 12

THE DREADS

$\mathcal{T}$his was one of those times I was living back at my mom's house. I had the big room in the basement this time because my sister had moved out to live with her boyfriend . . . I think. Honestly, all these episodes could be in the completely wrong order, but this is how I remember it.

I was downstairs in my room, looking at myself in the mirror. Sounds vain, I know, but we all do it. So, yeah, that's what I was doing.

"So, I have to give you this guy's number." My sister came barreling down the stairs and into the bedroom.

"What?" I asked, turning away from my reflection.

She pulled out her phone and showed me a picture of this light-skinned black guy with long dreads. I don't usually go for guys with dreads, but that man was beautiful. He had a chiseled jawline and big, dark brown eyes. He was handsome and the dreads didn't bother me so much when I looked at him. The longer I looked at him, the more I realized he looked familiar.

"I think I know him," I said as I handed my sister her phone back.

"Maybe. His name is Dreads. He went to Georgia Springs High School."

Okay . . . that's not his real name, but certainly you didn't think I was gonna slip up this time. And that's not the real name of the high school we went to either. Good luck, amateur sleuths. I know you'll probably figure it out. My old roommate would. Just please don't go harassing people. Back to the story.

"Oh, yeah. I think I remember him. He was a couple grades ahead of me. So, why do you have to give me his number?"

"We were at work and I was going through my pictures and Dreads stopped me when we got to one of you and asked who you were. I told him you were my sister and showed him more pictures of you and he was like 'shawty got dat ass' and then he asked me to give you his number." My sister was smiling ear to ear. "Don't you think he's cute?"

"Yeah, he's attractive." I tried to act cool about it, but that man was sexy. "Why didn't you just give him my number?"

"I tried, but he said he wanted it to be up to you if y'all talked."

"Well, isn't that thoughtful. Give me the number."

* * *

It was a couple of days later when I finally texted Dreads. We talked back and forth for a little bit and decided to hang out the following weekend. I was staying at Biff's for the weekend, which was not a total shocker. When he arrived at Biff's, it's a wonder I didn't attack him right then and there. He looked like a whole fucking meal. His smile was contagious, and he even brought dessert. Crown Royal Apple.

We clicked instantly in person and the three of us went to Edgewood to bar hop. Apparently, he and I made out all night. At least that's what Biff told me. I do remember doing something naughty with Dreads on her couch once we got back for the night.

"Shhhh," I said to him as I held my finger up to my lips.

He gave me that crooked, man-who-just-got-laid smile. "Why you telling me to shh?"

"You can't tell my sister."

He started cracking up. My sister had hooked us up, but I'm sure she wasn't expecting us to actually hook up so quickly. Neither of us ever told my sister what an amazing matchmaker she was, but I guess it's too late now. She's probably reading this sentence at this very moment and is going to send me a text in 3 . . . 2 . . . 1.

And now I've told all of you, so *insert shoulder shrug emoji*

* * *

ANOTHER NIGHT, the three of us went to Edgewood, and Biff's roommate joined us. We all met at some pretty quiet bar—as quiet as bars can get. We were drinking draanks, talking, and taking pictures. I don't know why I was chosen, but as we left that particular bar, a magical, wonderful man appeared. He presented me with a sash then smiled and disappeared. I looked down at the sash and it read 'bride to be'.

I wasn't a 'bride to be', but it was a sash. I had to put it on, right? Well, it doesn't matter if it was wrong, because I put it on anyway. The four of us headed to the next bar and when we got inside, the craziest thing happened. People started smiling at me as soon as we made eye contact. I received congratulations repeatedly. And get this—free drinks!

My free-booze-filled brain couldn't decipher what had happened between bar number one and bar number two.

That is, until I looked down and remembered I had put on a sash. A magical sash. I was a 'bride to be'.

Later that night, Dreads and I walked out of a bar, following Biff and her roommate. We were hand in hand when the doorman stopped us.

"Congratulations, man," he said to Dreads, looking at him and then smiling at me.

Dreads stopped and looked at the man with the most confused expression I had ever seen him wear. "For what?" he asked, his voice curt.

The man looked at me and my sash. Before he could answer, Dreads looked back at me and remembered our new best friend: the sash that had been getting us free drinks all night.

"Oh yeah," he said as he shook his head and tugged on my arm. "Come on."

"Maybe not congratulations?" I heard the door man murmur as we hurried past him.

I cracked up laughing on the way to the car. That poor man probably thought Dreads was ashamed of his soon-to-be wife or was annoyed with the upcoming nuptials altogether.

I still have that sash. It's hidden away in a secret place just waiting to use its magical powers for evil once again.

* * *

WHEN DREADS and I were dating, he didn't have a place of his own. Now, I couldn't complain because I was living with my mom. Even though he too was staying at his mom's house, he had it much better than I did. I'm not sure what his mom did for a living—I'm still not entirely convinced she wasn't a secret spy or superhero—but she would be gone for weeks or even months at a time and he'd have the whole house to himself.

One evening, I drove over to his house—well, to her house, I guess, but you get the point—to have dinner and spend the night. Turns out Mama Dreads had some amazing neighbors because I almost got my ass beat by a man with a cane just because I pulled into her driveway.

I parked the car and looked over out the window. The older man was walking down the sidewalk toward the house and giving me an evil glare. I didn't know I was getting *the look*, so I just smiled and got out of the car. I slung my bag over my shoulder and heard someone holler 'hey!' I looked over at the man and I could tell he was walking over to me with purpose, but he wasn't going very fast.

"Hey! Hey!" I heard again.

I don't know why, but my heart started pounding and I started wondering what the fuck I did.

"What are you doing?"

I started questioning if I was supposed to be there as I hurried up the driveway and banged on the front door.

"Excuse me! Young lady!"

I couldn't pound on the door quick enough. Finally, Dreads opened the door. He leaned forward to give me a kiss, but I ran past him and shut the door.

"Hey!" I heard faintly as the door slammed closed.

Dreads chuckled. "What are you doing?"

"I've gotta pee," I lied.

I quickly threw my bag down and walked to the bathroom, while unzipping my pants. The doorbell rang.

Dreads had walked into the kitchen. "Hey, Cole? Can you get that?"

"Nope. In the bathroom," I hollered as I locked myself in. Dreads was going to have to deal with the evil cane man alone.

I heard the front door open and some mumbling as I pretended to pee. After I heard the door shut and one set of footsteps walk past the hall bathroom toward the kitchen, I decided the coast was clear. I stood up, pulled up my pants, and washed my hands before joining Dreads in the kitchen.

"Who was that?" I asked innocently.

"Oh, just the neighbor. He said he didn't recognize your car and he's just trying to keep an eye on the house for Ma."

"Doesn't he know you're home? Your car is in the driveway?"

Dreads stopped cooking and looked up at me, grinning. "Yeah. He told me I'd better use protection."

Maybe Evil Cane Man wasn't so bad after all. Maybe he was just Mama Dreads sidekick.

* * *

NOT MUCH ELSE INTERESTING happened between Dreads and me. We dated for a few months and then it just didn't pan out. I wasn't the one and all of that shit I've heard time and time again. He wanted to try and work things out with his ex, so it was a goodbye to me. It wouldn't have been that bad except for the fact that he pretty much dumped me on Christmas Eve. However, he did give me his hoodie that I would always steal and a little decoration that says, 'there's only one thing better than a bottle of wine: two bottles of wine'. I still have that hoodie and that decorative sign.

Unbeknownst to me, Dreads blocked me on Snapchat. I figured this out because one day, about a year later, I got a notification saying, 'Dreads has added you on Snapchat'. When was I gone? Anyway, we got to talking and we still got along really well. He was no longer working on things with his ex and I was in a dry spell, so *hey hey hey, what's up?*

The whole friends with benefits thing happened for the

longest. We were really cool with each other, had a great time, cracked jokes, ate food, had sex. It was all pretty good shit. Of course, it had to come to an end.

I texted Dreads a few times without a response. It wasn't like him, so I hit him up and basically told him if he was no longer interested in what we were doing to just tell me that. That's when he told me he had a girlfriend. I was cool with it and respected it. I was only slightly pissed that he didn't just tell me that before he started ignoring me, but that, I could get over.

About a month later, Dreads posted a picture of some girl I assumed to be his girlfriend on Instagram. A couple weeks after that, another picture. A few months passed after the second sighting and there were no more pictures of the girl, despite Dreads being pretty active on his social media.

It was Christmas time and I had taken a week off work for the holidays. I was chilling at my dad's house when Dreads and I started chatting back and forth on Snapchat. I was bored and figured, *what the hay*. I could chill with Dreads. I asked him if he still had a girl and his response was 'does it matter lol'.

I pretty much assumed that meant yes, but I'd been wrong before. We tried to come up with a good time to hang out at some point during the break. Everything he said he had to do didn't include girlfriend plans, so at that point, I assumed they must have broken up.

Probably the last night I was going to be in town, Dreads and I were about to make some concrete plans. For some reason, he kept asking me to meet him at his dad's place. Now mind you, at that point he had his own apartment. A whole apartment. And he wanted me to meet him at his dad's spot? Why?

Me: I figured the whole point of us hanging out was to have some drinks and chill. If I'm gonna drink, I'm not about to drive back to my dad's house. And clearly we aren't gonna stay the night at your pops's place. Obviously, my apartment isn't going to work. (I lived in Athens at the time. I was visiting family in Dallas for the holidays). Why is it you're trying so hard to not hang out at your place?

Dreads: *My girl is living with me. Is that too much for you?*

Yes. Yes, it is.

* * *

YEAH . . . Dreads and I haven't seen each other since. At least, not in real life. I see him on Instagram and Snapchat occasionally. And I know he sees me. I get notifications every once in a while saying Dreads has screenshotted my picture.

You know what they say, if you like what you see.

EPISODE 13

THE FRIEND

*T*his is a short short story about a friend of my once-upon-a-time brother-in-law. This friend tried to put me in the friend zone after we hung out as more than friends for weeks and then this friend turned out to be a major fuckboy.

I met this one at my sister's wedding. He was good friends with the groom, who is now no longer my brother-in-law, but that is not my story to tell, so we'll leave that right there.

The wedding was small and held at my grandmother's house. I wasn't able to drink too much because I had to drive two and a half hours back to Athens when it was over, so I could be up at the ass crack of dawn for work the next day. Even with the lack of alcohol, I still got the party started by being the only one on the dance floor. I dragged Biff out onto the floor with me after a song or two. I can't dance to save my life, but trust me, I will dance regardless.

Friend caught my eye the moment he walked in. He was lean with a medium chocolate complexion and just enough stubble on his face without looking like he needed to shave.

His smile was contagious, and though he didn't join me on the dance floor, I caught him watching me from time to time.

I knew I couldn't leave without saying something to him, so I got my sister to grab him for me. I got his number in a real cool kind of way and then I headed out.

A couple weeks passed and we eventually hung out. We hung out on the weekends for a few weeks after that, maybe a month. There's not too much to share here except Friend started distancing himself. He got all weird and the last weekend I tried to hang out with him, he told me I could come over, but he had to go to his church's Bible study. He said I was welcome to go with him for the night, but I couldn't sleep over. That was weird, coming from him. Bible study is great and all, but if you're trying to friend zone me or kick me out of your bed at four in the morning, don't do it with church. Be a man and say we aren't going to work out, don't use The Man Upstairs to do your dirty work. I'm all for church, but it ain't for that. Uh uh. I told him I would pass and that was that. I didn't really hear from him again. That is, until his sister had her baby. I knew how excited Friend was to be an uncle, so when I saw the news, I texted him to congratulate him. Apparently he took that the wrong way, like I was trying to get back with him or some shit. He sent me this long ass, passive aggressive as hell message back and I lost it. I saw red and I sent him a long ass message back. Mine wasn't too friendly either. I know because I showed it to my friend and she blushed.

I wish I still had that message so I could share it here, but I don't. Just know I added another fuckboy onto the relation-shit list.

EPISODE 14

THE HOME FRY

*O*kay, so remember the guy who offered me some french fries at the end of Sorry's episode? Well, if you don't, go back and read the last few paragraphs. Yeah . . . that one. This is his episode. It's not a very long one, but it's shitty nonetheless.

I met Home Fry through one of my best friends' husbands. It was a warm summer night in Athens. Most of the students were gone until the fall semester. The summer was when the real grown-ups went out to party downtown. A few of us went and grabbed a couple of drinks at one of the local bars. Afterward, my best friend, her husband, and I ended up in the townhome complex across the street from mine.

My best friend's husband—we'll call him Jason—knew some people who lived there. It was a couple and their roommate. The husband in the couple and the roommate both worked with Jason. We all chilled out on their back porch, taking shots and shooting the shit.

The roommate was Home Fry. He wasn't my typical type,

if I could say I had one. He was average height, white, had shaggy brown hair, and glasses. He was the kind of guy who wore a fisher's shirt, khaki shorts, and tan flip flops. Even not really having a type, Home Fry was definitely not it.

He was different though and funny, and he had a great smile. And let's cut to it, living across the street, he was convenient dick. We didn't hook up that night, but I definitely gave him the eyes and asked my friend to get the details on his love life from her husband.

There were a few times here and there when we all got together, along with some other friends during that summer. We all hung out at Home Fry's place, went to bars downtown, and drank cold beers at local breweries.

One of the times we were all out together was the night Sorry and I got into that huge argument. I'm not going to recap the whole night, but right before we headed to the pizza place where I "lost" my wallet, some other shit happened.

We were leaving the bar when Jason's friend decided to get in a fight. Not Home Fry, the other co-worker . . . the married one. I have no clue what the hell happened or how the shit even started. I just know I was in the middle of talking to Home Fry and he just vanished. It was like I hadn't been talking to anyone. One second he was standing in front of me, and the next, there was a gust of wind and he was gone.

He dashed over to where his roommate was in a real fight with someone. Like, a physical altercation. I looked over and he was on the ground. Fists were flying, fingers were grabbing, and shoes were getting tossed.

My friend's husband joined in briefly and it quickly de-escalated. My friend, the co-worker's wife, and I were all just standing on the sidewalk, in shock. Our mouths were open and our eyes were huge. I don't know what the other two were thinking, but I was trying not to bust out laughing.

I mean, seriously, it was a large group of grown ass men essentially all throwing temper tantrums at once.

Suddenly, Home Fry was standing back in front of me.

"Are you okay?" I asked him.

"Yeah, but I lost my glasses."

I looked at him and it was just in that moment I realized his face was bare.

"That sucks ass." I shook my head.

I owned glasses. I was supposed to wear them, but I hardly ever did. But I knew how expensive those bitches are.

"Yeah." His hand went to the back of his neck. He looked back over toward where the fight had taken place.

"Can you see?"

"Barely." He sighed. "I just don't know where they went. They should be over there somewhere . . ."

"So, what happened?"

"I don't know what started it, but when I saw co-worker get pushed to the ground, I knew I had to help."

I rolled my eyes. "I guess."

"He shit himself."

"WHAT?"

"Yeah. He shit himself. He said when he saw that first fist come flying toward his face, he just couldn't stop the little shit from coming out."

And that's when I lost it. I laughed so hard, I'm surprised I didn't shit *myself*.

After that was when we started walking toward the pizza place and well, you know the rest of that story.

* * *

ONE NIGHT I was over at Home Fry's place, chilling with him and the married couple. We'll call the wife M and now, I'll finally give you something to call the married co-worker: C.

Anyway, after a calmer night out, I ended up at their house. My best friend and her husband had left downtown earlier in the night and the other people we were with departed soon after that. For some reason, M, C, and Home Fry wanted to take a taxi home. Why they didn't want to use Uber or Lyft was beyond me. However, I told them if we took a taxi, there was no way I was paying for that shit.

They insisted on the taxi after we grabbed some food, for nostalgia's sake. So, we flagged one down and hopped inside. On the way over, they insisted I go to their house and hang out with them longer. I wasn't really tired, and I'll never be too old for free booze, so I agreed. If I wanted to go home, I literally just had to walk across the street.

When we got to their house, the driver told them it was thirty dollars. I got my ass out of that seat and up to their door really quick. I told them I wasn't paying for that mess, though I was just drunk enough that they probably could have guilt-tripped me into helping them pay.

After paying the over-priced fee, they opened the door and in we went. We played some games and drank some more liquor. C went to bed first. He was beyond drunk and there was no way he was gonna make it later than he did.

The three of us chilled in the living room with their dogs for probably an hour longer. Then M was ready to go to bed.

"You're too drunk to walk across the street. You're staying here." She was looking at me.

"What?" I asked.

"I'm not letting you leave. I will not have your kidnapping on my hands."

"Okay, Mom."

She laughed. "Come on. I'll show you where you can sleep."

The three of us walked up the stairs. Home Fry dipped off into his room and M and I continued walking down the short hall.

"Here you go." She opened a door into an empty bedroom.

There was a twin-size mattress on the floor, but beyond that, the room was bare.

"I'll go grab you a couple of blankets." She skipped back down the hall, like she was excited to have a house guest.

I plopped down on the mattress and waited for her to return. It didn't take long, and M came back with two thin blankets for me. She handed them over and then left the room, shutting the door behind her.

I laid back onto the mattress and covered myself up with the blankets. Just as my eyes were adjusting to the blackness, the door creaked open. I lifted my head, fully expecting to see M.

"Want to come to my room?"

It was Home Fry.

"Yeah," I whisper-yelled.

I jumped off the mattress and followed him back to his room. We watched probably half of a movie before we started hooking up. I was drunk, but Home Fry was definitely a good kisser. I stand by that.

I don't remember much of the sex, but I do remember waking up to something licking my feet. For a split second, I thought it was Home Fry trying to have some morning fun. Then I realized his arms were around my shoulders. Unless he knew how to somehow have his head at my feet and his arms at my shoulders, I knew it couldn't be him.

I opened my eyes and looked down, trying not to scream. When I realized it was his dog, I was glad I had made the decision not to kick at my attacker. Then another thought occurred to me. How much had the dog seen? The door had been closed all night.

Embarrassed, (yes, I was horrified that the dog had watched us fuck) I sat up to look for my pants. When I took in the state of the room, I was no longer embarrassed. Not for me anyway. There was shit everywhere. Dirty laundry, empty beer cans, old plates, and pizza—yes, there was pizza still sitting in a box. The fact that the dog chose licking my feet over eating leftover food should tell you how old that shit was.

Somehow, I managed to find my pants. I lifted off my ass to grab them and before I could reach them, Home Fry pulled me back to where he laid. He kissed my lips sweetly and said, "We gotta do that again."

I simply smiled at him and said, "Sure."

Getting out of the bed completely, I searched for my pants again. I found them quicker this time and pulled them up my legs. I looked back at him to say bye, but his eyes were closed and I assumed he had fallen back asleep.

I walked the short distance back to my house, praying that no one I knew saw me crossing the street in what were clearly last night's clothes, now covered in dog hair.

I made it back home safely. No one saw me and I quickly took the clothes off, tossed them in the wash and threw myself in the shower.

A few weeks passed and I was pretty horny. Dog hair and stale pizza aside . . . Remember I told you, being across the street equals convenient dick. He wasn't messy in the dick department and we could totally hook up at my house. I got his number from M and sent him a text telling him it was Cole and that M gave me his number.

He never responded.

I sent another text a couple of days later asking him if he wanted to hangout. I was a girl with needs, okay.

No response.

I never heard from him again and for all I know he suffocated under all the clothes piled up in his room. Or he ate that pizza.

EPISODE 15

❧

THE ZOMBIE

 here do I begin with this one, huh? I started writing this story almost twenty years ago. Remember the lanky kid with the basketball at the beginning of this book? Yeah, this episode is about him.

I met Zombie when I was eight years old. My family had just moved to Georgia from Germany. My dad had been in the Air Force, and after completing his service, he and my mom decided to move back to where they grew up. Georgia was as good a place as anywhere to raise two girls and eventually a boy when my brother came along.

While my parents looked for a house, we stayed with my aunt and uncle on my dad's side. For the remaining few months of third grade, I went to an elementary school where I met Zombie and Biff. We were fast friends and stayed that way for a long time.

Biff and I remained closer than Zombie and I did. Though Biff and I went to different middle schools, we still remained friends, seeing each other at orchestra events. Yes, we were both orcha-dorks, and proud of it. She played bass and I played violin. However, Zombie performed his first disappearing act after I left that elementary school for another for fourth and fifth grade.

It was my senior year of high school when Zombie and I reconnected. I remember walking from one building to the next—my high school was an old college, so it had an open campus—when I spotted Zombie standing awkwardly against the bell tower. He was still wearing glasses and was still the tallest guy I'd seen, but now, in high school, I was really looking up. At 6'9", he hardly noticed my 5'1" frame staring at him.

"Hey!" I hollered up. "Do you remember me?"

Zombie looked down, and after a few seconds of taking me in, his lips turned up into a huge dazzling smile. He remembered me and we clicked instantly. It was like we were eight years old again—best friends.

Though I was in a relationship with Pup at the time, the friendship between Zombie and me turned into romantic feelings. Pup and I ended for a time, and Zombie and I decided to give things a go.

The first date we went on was definitely one for the books. I'm not saying it was amazing and super romantic because, trust me, it wasn't. I mean how romantic can you be at seventeen years old anyway? It was definitely memorable though.

Anyway, so we went to dinner at Chili's. The dinner part went pretty well. We always had a good time and were comfortable with each other. Complete goofballs. We'd known each other for years, right? So, there was no awkward conversation or anything like that.

After we ate and paid the bill, Zombie said he needed to use the restroom before we left. He got up from the table and I played a game of Snake on my flip phone until he returned. *I'm not that old, I swear. Snake was still a thing at that point in time. Technology has just progressed . . . a lot.*

I had played probably three games of Snake when I realized Zombie still wasn't back. I started to look around the room and couldn't find him. The wait staff kept passing by our table, I guess wondering why I hadn't left yet; my date was clearly gone. Perhaps they figured he had either ditched me or I was waiting on date number two for the evening.

I thought maybe the food had upset his stomach and he needed some extra time in the restroom, so I played another game on my phone. Afterward, when Zombie still hadn't returned, I started to get worried. I grabbed onto the arm of one of the waiters and told him my date had gone to the restroom and hadn't come back.

"Can you please go check on him and make sure nothing happened?"

The waiter looked at me as if I had just asked the most outrageous question in the world. I mean, maybe a grown man going to check on another grown man was a weird thing to do, but I didn't care.

"What's he look like?" he asked.

"He's tall, dark, and handsome." I smiled at the waiter.

He just stared back at me without saying a word.

Trying to do better in my description, I continued. "I'm serious. He's 6'9. He's black. And he's good-looking. Can't miss him."

The waiter shook his head. "Sure. I'll be right back," he said.

A few moments later, the waiter returned, but there was no giant trailing behind him. "I'm sorry, ma'am. There was no one in there."

The corner of my lip lifted slightly. "Okay, thanks for checking."

Before he walked off, the waiter looked at me with sad eyes. Those eyes that said 'Damn. That asshole must have climbed out of the bathroom window and left this poor girl all alone.'

Honestly, that's what I thought. I mean, how could I have missed a gangly teenager who's six foot nine go out the front door? Then again, how could a gangly teenager who's six foot nine crawl out of a bathroom window?

With my pride barely hanging on and tears being force-fully held in, I walked out of Chili's and toward my car.

When I got to my car, who was leaning against the passenger side? Zombie. I just stared at him without saying a word. He put his phone in his pocket and looked back at me.

"What?" he asked with a goofy grin on his face.

"Where did you go? It's been thirty minutes. I was worried about you."

"I couldn't find you."

"I was literally at the table we ate at." I crossed my arms.

"I couldn't find the table."

* * *

WHEN ZOMBIE and I started college, things changed. We were still dating, but I wasn't so sure things were going to end in happily ever after. The two of us went to different universities. I attended school in Georgia, and he went to a school in Tennessee on a basketball scholarship. The distance put a wedge between us. The fact that I still had feelings for my true best friend at the time, Pup, didn't help either.

There was one night, Zombie and I got into our first real argument. I was going out with some of my friends and so was he, but there was a problem. At least, there was a problem for him. He thought that since we weren't going out together, I shouldn't be going out. I. Me. Just me. He had no problem with him going out without me, but this girl, yeah, she couldn't go out without him. That obviously was an issue.

I remember walking up one of the big hills on campus, talking on the phone with Zombie as I made my way to the party, because yes, I was going out. He was clearly drunk already and wasn't making any sense, but I could tell he was going off on a rant because I was walking to a party he didn't want me to go to. I was yelling his name, trying to get him to listen when I heard a click. The bitch hung up on me. He didn't answer my calls or texts the rest of the night.

Turns out, Zombie got his wish anyway. I didn't end up attending the party. My friends and I got there, but never went in. It was a white fraternity party. My friends and I, who were all black, showed up at the entrance. One of the drunken frat brothers asked us what we wanted. My friend said so-and-so had invited her and said she could bring some friends.

"But you're black!" he slurred.

We all looked at him, stunned that the words had actually come out of his mouth.

He started laughing while we stared, music thudding behind him. "So-and-so would never invite you."

He was still laughing as we walked away.

"What did they want?" I heard someone ask the guy behind us.

"Those black girls thought they were gonna get into the party. We don't take no black girls here!" The two of them howled with laughter.

I tried to call Zombie when I got back to my room to tell him what happened, but he never answered. There was a picture of him on Facebook the next day, drunk at whatever party he had gone to.

* * *

THINGS ENDED NOT TOO long after that. I just knew it wasn't going to work. We wanted different things and we expected things of each other that we weren't willing to give. I wrote Zombie a letter and then took a picture of it and sent it to him. I told him we needed to talk when he got out of class. I told him I had written him a letter and I wanted to read it to him and discuss things.

It was rare, at the time, to have a phone that could zoom in on a picture. *Freaky, I know.* I didn't know or had just completely forgotten, that Zombie had a phone that could zoom in on pictures. Apparently, he had zoomed in on the photo I sent him and read the letter before I had a chance to call him.

That night, I tried to call him over and over again, but never got him on the phone. I had told him in the letter I didn't think we would work. I was honest about my feelings. I wrote about how we were in college and how it didn't seem we wanted the same experiences. I told him how I still had feelings for Pup, and though things with Pup had gone nowhere, I didn't feel like it was right to continue a relationship with him when my heart was elsewhere. I had been in love with Pup, for goodness sakes. I left that part out.

After trying desperately to reach Zombie, I was just about to give up for the day when his twin brother sent me a text message. He said Zombie didn't want to speak with me and that I was wrong for what I did. Zombie had really fallen for me the way he had never seen his brother do. The way I went about things was mean and I should stop trying to get in touch with Zombie.

I didn't know his phone could zoom in on pictures!

* * *

A FEW WEEKS passed and I started seeing Zombie be more

active on his Facebook. I liked a couple things on his page, commented here and there, and nothing. However, I thought nothing was better than my comments being deleted. He even liked one of them once. Things seemed to be improving. Maybe, eventually, we could be friends again. We had known each other since we were eight, right?

I can't remember what it was he posted, but I commented on the post like I had done a few times before. I went on about my day and when I got to my room after class that night, I opened my large purple laptop and logged into Facebook. I had a few notifications, but when I saw one stating Zombie had commented on something, I was elated! Was he actually speaking to me now?

I pulled up the post and scrolled down to the comment I had left. The first response wasn't from Zombie at all. It was from one of his friends.

"Isn't that the chick who sucked on your big toe?"

"Haha! Yeah, boy, she sucked on the big toe real good."

I deleted my comment, deleting those responses, and didn't speak to Zombie again for years.

* * *

I WAS in my third year of college when Zombie reached out to me. It didn't take much to bring us close together again. We both apologized for being dumb freshmen and continued our friendship like nothing bad had ever happened between us. Water under the bridge.

I was no longer with Pup but was in my relationshit or situationship or whatever the fuck you want to call it with B at the time. Zombie was dating some cute Hispanic girl. She really was gorgeous, but—and there's a big but—she really was crazy. I can't tell you the number of times Zombie called me telling me the girl had lost her marbles again. She threw a stapler at him one time, cut up his shoes with scissors, and burned him with her curling iron.

Needless to say, they eventually broke up. She sent me a long ass message on Facebook after they broke up saying some things about Zombie. I can't remember exactly what it said, but it was somewhat kind; she just wanted to know some things about Zombie. I guess she knew I really was just the friend, but I wasn't about to get in the middle of her losing her marbles . . . again. Deleted. Acted like I never saw the message.

* * *

AFTER COLLEGE, Zombie, Biff and I hung out quite a bit. I was staying with my mom, Biff was staying with hers, and Zombie was staying with his. It was like we were in high school again, except this time we were old enough to drink liquor legally and stay up as late as we wanted.

Mostly, we all hung out together, but a few times, it was just me and Zombie. We eventually hooked up. Yes, it's true. We didn't sleep together until we were both twenty-two years old. It wasn't a memorable experience, because I can't remember when or how it happened. But even though the first time we hooked up wasn't something to put in the books, literally, there were a couple of times that were.

One of Biff's friends hosted a house party. Biff, Zombie and I decided to go. My sister and one of her guy friends were chilling with us that night. The two of them looked at each other and figured they would go too. It worked out in our favor because my sister didn't really like drinking at the time, so built-in DD!

We got to the party and all went inside. My sister's friend was a lightweight, so after a couple of drinks, the two of them went outside to chill in her car until Zombie, Biff, and I were ready to go. I don't know how we all managed to get so drunk in such a short amount of time, but we accomplished it.

Biff was chilling with her friends when Zombie and I stumbled up the stairs, hand in hand. We found a room and knocked. No one answered, so Zombie opened the door and there was no one inside. The room was trashed and looked like it was a space just for storage. There was a bed, but surely no one slept in here.

We shrugged our shoulders and walked in. We shut and locked the door behind us and quickly started making out. Have you ever seen a 6'9" man and a 5'1" woman make out? That in and of itself is pretty entertaining. People in high school used to make fun of us all the time, saying Zombie had to bend down at a ninety-degree angle to give me a hug.

Anyway, we were making out and eventually ended up on the floor. We couldn't have gotten on the bed because there was shit all over it. Not literal shit—we'll get to that later—but you know what I mean. As we were kissing, about to take things to the next level, I remembered something.

"I'm on my period," I said through slobbery kissing.

"So," Zombie countered as he started undoing my jeans. His pants were already off.

"But I have a tampon in," I panted.

There were no words said after that. In one swift movement, Zombie had my pants and underwear off and pulled out my tampon. He tugged on that little white string and out the thing came. He threw it in the room somewhere and into pound town we went.

As soon as we were done, I told Zombie we had to go. I didn't have a backup tampon and we were clearly far too gone in our drunkenness and needed to get back to the house. Zombie agreed and we went downstairs to find Biff.

After finding Biff, we realized we couldn't find a few

other important things, specifically my wallet, my cell phone, and Zombie's shoes. They were all gone. We searched inside for a few minutes, but when we found Zombie asleep, standing against a wall, we knew it was time to go. Biff said she would talk to her friend tomorrow about finding our stuff.

We woke Zombie up and attempted to get him to walk out the front door. He couldn't figure out how to get his size fifteen feet to move, so it took me, Biff, and my sister to basically carry him to the car. It was more of a drag, but you get the point. My sister's friend was sitting in the passenger seat, passed out. He literally had two drinks. Two small drinks.

There was no way Zombie was going to be able to drive home that night and his car was at my mom's house. My mom loved Zombie, so I didn't think she'd have a problem with him staying there for the night. After dropping off my sister's friend and pulling the car over so I could puke, we finally made it home. I went into my mom's room after Biff, my sister, and I again carried Zombie through the front door. I woke her up and told her Zombie needed to crash on the couch because he was too drunk to drive.

"Okay," she whispered without opening her eyes.

"Mom? Did you hear me?"

"Yes." She started to roll over.

"Mom? Zombie is staying here, okay? There's going to be a very large man on the couch when you wake up."

"Okay, I hear you." Her voice trailed off and she went back to sleep. She never opened her eyes.

After walking out of my mom's room, I saw my sister and Biff standing over Zombie in the office. There was a small—and I mean *tiny*—couch in the office. The couch wasn't meant for sleeping. It was more for decoration.

"We tried to wake him up to move him to the living room, but he won't budge," my sister said.

If you had seen Zombie on this couch, you would have died with laughter. It really was a small couch and Zombie was 6'9". His torso was basically the only thing lying on the furniture. The rest of him was on the floor. However, he looked like he was resting peacefully.

"Zombie?" I tried nudging him, but my sister was right. He wouldn't move.

"Just leave him there," I said.

The three of us headed up the stairs to get some rest.

The next morning, Biff and I woke up and headed downstairs. My mom was cooking in the kitchen and when we rounded the corner to join her, she started cracking up.

"Did you see how Zombie is sleeping?"

"Yes," I said.

"Why didn't you put him on one of the bigger couches?" she asked.

"We tried, but that's where he landed, and he wouldn't move."

My mom shook her head. "He scared the crap out of me this morning."

"You don't remember me telling you he needed to sleep here, huh?" I asked.

"No." My mom looked confused.

"Yeah, I figured you wouldn't. I came in there and told you twice he was too drunk to drive anywhere."

"I don't doubt you did. You know how I get when I'm asleep."

I nodded.

My mom continued, "Did you know he sleeps with his eyes open."

Biff and I started laughing. "Yeah, I did. His eyelids won't cover his eyes." This was said in all seriousness and yes, this is #facts.

About an hour later, Zombie woke up. He came and sat

with Biff and me at the bar in the kitchen and asked about last night. We gave him the quick version and disclosed to him that he no longer had his shoes. He looked down at his feet and it was like he noticed for the first time his feet had no shoes.

It was the funniest thing watching him leave and get into his car shoeless. Zombie said when he got home that morning, his mom looked him up and down. She asked him where his shoes were, and Zombie told her his shoes were gone. He said his mom simply shook her head and continued doing what she was doing.

Later that day, Biff's friend texted her. He said he found Zombie's shoes but didn't find my wallet or my cell phone. Stolen, I was sure. He also said the house was a mess and it took them hours to clean. Someone had even left a bloody tampon in his bedroom. I wonder who would do such a gross thing. I guess it wasn't a messy storage room after all. Whoops.

* * *

REMEMBER when I said earlier we'd get back to shit on the bed? Well, here's that story.

Like I told you, Zombie and I used to hook up . . . a lot. My mom was a heavy sleeper, by her own admission in that last story. So sometimes, Zombie would come over, we'd chill and watch TV and then wind up in my bed.

There was one night in particular when I put in all the work. By that, I mean I was on top the entire time. I'm not complaining, but that fact is going to be important here in a minute.

Zombie and I had sex, we chilled a bit longer and then I walked him to the door. After he left, I hopped in the shower, fixed myself a drink, and then sat on the futon in my room and watched TV for about an hour or so.

When I got tired, I stripped my clothes off and climbed into the bed. I had lain there for a few minutes when I started smelling something awful. I couldn't quite pinpoint it, but there was definitely a smell. Had I farted and not even noticed it? Surely not.

I tried to ignore the smell and closed my eyes. However, it kept wafting up my nostrils. I got out of the bed and turned the lights back on. I pulled the sheets down and low and behold, there was the source. There was a small, but very obvious, shit stain on my sheets. It was the kind of shit stain you'd expect to see in a pair of tighty whities, but here it was, embedded onto my sheets.

Over the past couple of weeks, I had noticed Zombie wasn't smelling completely fresh, but I couldn't figure it out. A strange smell followed him and lingered for a little bit when he left a room. Staring at the stain on my sheets, I had figured it out. Zombie wasn't wiping his ass. That had to be it.

I confided in Biff after I washed the sheets and asked her what I should do.

"I should tell him, right?" I asked. "He's our friend. He should know?"

"Yes, I think you should tell him."

Now, I had washed the sheets, but the stain didn't come out. I washed them again, just to be sure, but the stain was still there. I had to do something disgusting. I put my nose up to the stain and phew! Though the stain was set, the smell had left. When I was reading this section for editing, I realized 'phew' could be taken as 'yuck, stinky.' So, I guess I should have clarified that I said 'phew' in relief.

Second round of editing: my editor stated I should have

used 'whew'. Fact about the author: needs help with words sometimes. *insert cheesy smiley emoji

The next time Zombie came over, I sat him down to break the news. We were sitting on the futon when I told him I had to share something important with him.

"Come here. I've got to show you something." I got up from the futon and Zombie followed me over to my bed.

I moved the sheets down and pointed to the stain.

"What's that?" Zombie asked, confused.

"It's a shit stain," I said bluntly.

"Ewww. Why are you showing me that?"

"It's from you."

"No, it's not."

"Zombie, it happened the last time we hooked up."

"You did that!" he accused me.

"But, Zombie, how could I have done that? I was on top the whole time!" (I told you that fact was going to be important later.)

"It wasn't me," Zombie said as he crossed his arms.

The rest of the night was pretty awkward, but I'm convinced he got the point. He never smelled funny again and there were never again shit sheets.

Try saying 'shit sheets' five times fast.

* * *

AFTER I MOVED to back to Athens, things were slightly different between Biff, Zombie, and me. We hung out when we could, but it wasn't as often as it was before. Zombie and Biff still lived in Atlanta, so there were times they hung out when I couldn't.

One day, after a party Biff had hosted at her house, Biff called me and told me Zombie was upset with me. She said he came to her house party and had called me a bitch.

"Excuse me? A what?" I asked her.

"A bitch. He said you were a bitch."

I was silent for a moment, trying to think back and see if I could remember ever doing anything mean to Zombie—recently, anyway. The whole breaking up over a letter sent in a picture and calling him out on the shit sheets was over and done with at that point.

Nothing. I could think of nothing.

"Why would he say that?"

"Well, one, he was drunk. He asked why you weren't at the party and I told him because you live in Athens and you had to work and blah blah blah. He then asked me if I talked to you anymore and I told him, well yeah, we're BFFLs. Then he got this sad look on his face and said that you only ever contact him when you want to hook up. He said you're a bitch and only use him for a booty call."

I was stunned. I hadn't talked to Zombie in a very long time. But then again, I guess that was the point he was making. I decided then that I wasn't going to hook up with Zombie anymore. This wasn't a decision made from spite. If he really felt that way, then we didn't need to hook up. His friendship meant a lot to me and I wasn't going to let sex get in the way of that. I needed to do a better job of being his friend. I didn't tell Zombie what Biff had relayed to me, and I did start communicating with him more, and we didn't hook up.

* * *

ZOMBIE and I started texting a lot more. He again became my best friend. We goofed around and cracked jokes. He would come to visit me in Athens and he was that guy friend who could sleep in my bed with me, no funny business, and it wasn't an issue.

Months and years passed, and my friends and family kept bringing up Zombie. 'You should date Zombie.' 'You should give him a chance.' 'Y'all would be so cute together.' 'He would treat you right.' 'The two of you are going to end up together.'

Zombie and I did make a pact when we were in high school that if the two of us were both single and 35, we would get married. It was cute, but it was like a joke. Surely, I'll have someone by the time I'm 35, right? But here I am knocking on 30's door and still alone, but that's beside the point. After I knew how Zombie really felt, I couldn't lead him on. I'd been there, done that, and it didn't work out. We worked as friends, not together, in a relationship.

In 2017, my friend was getting married and asked me to be one of her bridesmaids. I was allowed a plus-one, and as the only single bridesmaid, I had to bring someone. I told Zombie about it and he begged me to please take him. He loved weddings and he would be my date. I rolled my eyes and asked him to be my date and he, of course, obliged.

Zombie showed up just in time. I really thought he was going to stand me up. I had been texting him all day, telling him about when to show up, how he should take an Uber from my house, what to wear, and so on and so forth. He didn't reply not once. I finally asked him if he was coming and still, he didn't answer. I told Biff what was going on and she tried to contact him. Nothing.

I was upset, but I wasn't that mad. I mean, there was one groomsman I had my eye on. I figured I could just dance the night away with him since Zombie was being a jerk. The bride, the other bridesmaids, and I were all hanging out and drinking in the bridal suite when the guests started arriving. We peeked out the window, trying to get a look at everyone. I was throwing back a shot when Katie, the bride, yelled over to me.

"Zombie's here."

I swallowed the Fireball in my mouth, almost choking. "What?"

She turned around and nodded her head with pursed lips. "Yup. He just got here."

I grabbed my phone and brightened the screen. No texts. The asshole just showed up. I was still going to dance the night away with sexy groomsman. I called Biff and let her know he showed and she could stop trying to contact him.

After the ceremony and pictures, I found Zombie at the reception. I showed him where we were sitting and then I laid into him. He apologized and I rolled my eyes and went on to have a good time.

I tried flirting with Sexy Groomsman after dinner, but Zombie was having no part of that. He box blocked me so hard. I was in the middle of talking to Sexy Groomsman, flirting up a storm, when Zombie joined our twosome and made it a threesome. He started talking to Sexy Groomsman, leaving me no room to interject. I walked away and found one of the guests, Jackie. She was in a relationship with one of the other groomsmen and pretty good friends with the groom.

"Do you have Sexy Groomsman's number?"

"What?" she asked me.

"Sexy Groomsman? Do you have his number?"

She looked at me with confusion dripping from her face. "But what about Zombie?"

"Huh?"

"What about Zombie? He really likes you. You should give him a chance."

Apparently the two of them had talked during cocktail hour, while the bridal party was taking pictures. I had known this woman all of 24 hours and Zombie had already gotten to her.

After the wedding, we all went out and partied hard. I finally got to flirt—distraction-free—with Sexy Groomsman when Zombie told me he was going to join some of the other guys from the wedding at a different bar. I told him to go for it and to text me when they left that bar, so we could meet up. He was staying at my house and wasn't from Athens. He was annoying, but he was my best friend and I had a responsibility for him for the weekend.

I'm not quite sure how I managed it, but I woke up in my own bed alone the next morning. After Zombie left the bar, the rest of the night was pretty blurry. I remember being in an Uber alone, getting dropped off in my neighborhood, stumbling down the street to my front door, and trying to break into my own house. I guess I couldn't find my keys because I distinctly remember using my credit cards to try and get into the house. Somehow, I managed to get in because the next thing I remember is waking up in the bed.

Beyond getting so drunk I couldn't remember how I got in my room, there was another issue. I was alone. Normally this would be a good thing, but there was no Zombie. I sat up in the bed and looked around. No Zombie. I went downstairs and still found no Zombie. I went back upstairs, found my phone and looked through it. There were no text messages from Zombie, no phone calls, nothing. I immediately tried calling him, but the phone went straight to voicemail. I waited about ten minutes and tried to call him again. I got the voicemail a second time.

I was worried, but I was exhausted. I set my alarm for forty-five minutes, put the ringer on loud, and placed the phone on the charger. After my alarm went off, I looked at my phone again and still had no form of contact from Zombie. I realized then, all his stuff was still in my room. We had stopped by after the wedding to change before we went out and everything he had brought in with him was still sitting in its place.

Despite my headache, I crawled out of my bed and put on some clothes and shoes. I didn't know where exactly I was going to go, but I planned on driving around Athens until I found Zombie or until he called me. When I opened my bedroom door, I heard a knock coming from the front door downstairs. My roommate was studying at the dining room table and she got up and answered the door. I had made it about halfway down the stairs when Zombie rounded the corner.

"Oh my gosh!" I whisper-yelled. "Where have you been?"

We walked up the stairs to my room. "Man," he started, "last night was crazy."

Once we were in my room, Zombie started gathering his things.

"Where have you been?" I asked him again, hands on hips. "I've been worried about you."

He didn't stop packing his stuff, but he answered my question. "Well, after we left that one bar, we went to Nameless Bar." He stopped momentarily to look at me. "Which is garbage by the way."

I rolled my eyes. "Well, I could have told you that."

"So, after that, we went to some other bars and I don't remember exactly what happened, but I ended up at some random white guy's apartment with Jackie and her boyfriend. Shit got crazy."

"What do you mean?"

"Nothing." He threw his bag over his shoulder. "I woke up this morning and realized my phone was dead. No one there had a charger I could use, so I walked around downtown Athens until CVS opened up. I bought a charger and went into one of the restaurants to charge my phone. Then I ordered an Uber and here we are."

"Why didn't you call or text me last night? You were supposed to let me know where you were going!"

"I'm sorry. I forgot." He put his sad face on.

"Fine." I crossed my arms. "Don't do it again."

"I promise. Look, I gotta go. Let me know when there's another wedding in Athens. I'll be your date."

"Mmhmm." I rolled my eyes

I walked Zombie down the stairs and out the front the door. When I came back in, I walked into the kitchen to make myself a cup of coffee. My roommate was still sitting at the table, studying.

"How was last night?" she asked.

"It was fun, but turned out to be a shit show." I turned around to face her to tell her more about the night.

That's when I noticed my bra and my purse sitting on the table.

"Why the heck is this down here?" I asked myself out loud.

"I brought it in here from outside," my roommate said with a laugh.

"What?" I asked her.

"Yeah, that stuff was on the front steps. When I got home this morning, I brought it in."

The purse was plausible. I had been digging around in it, trying to find stuff to break into my house, but the bra? I don't remember taking that off. I thanked my roommate, grabbed my things, and walked back upstairs, forgetting the cup of coffee. I just needed sleep.

Shit did get crazy last night.

* * *

I COULDN'T TELL you when it happened or why it happened, but it happened. For some reason, I decided to take everyone up on their advice. I had a crush on Zombie. He started growing on me in a relationshipy kind of way. He was looking better, his jokes were funnier, and he started making things get all warm in my nether regions.

I told my dad I liked Zombie and he was thrilled. My dad loved Zombie. He couldn't tell you why, I couldn't tell you why, since they had only met a couple of times, but it was the reality of things.

"I knew it!" Biff said when I told her I liked him and was willing to give him a try. It was the answer I got from everyone who had ever told me to go for it, back when I trusted my gut. I should have continued listening to it, but I didn't do it. If I had, we wouldn't have any more of a story here.

After a few weeks of deciding I *like* liked Zombie, I told him. He grinned from ear to ear and asked 'really?' We started hanging out a lot more and after a little more than a month, we made things official. At least I thought we had. Biff had asked him at one point if we were a couple now and he said yes, so I thought it was pretty clear. Anyway, we'll get into that later.

We were together for a few weeks before he ghosted on me—the first time. He was supposed to come to Athens to visit me one night after work. I was working the overnight shift at my job but was going to be home early in the morning. I had taken the next night off, that way we could have some time together. The plan was for him to meet me at the house before I left, so we could eat dinner and then he was going to chill and sleep while I was at work.

The day came and I hadn't heard from him. I tried calling and texting, but I heard nothing. It was like Katie's wedding all over again. The night went on and I had to leave for work. I took the spare key with me and called Zombie again. He didn't answer and I sent him a text telling him to call me when he could, and he could meet me at work so I could give him the spare key. I worked the entire night and didn't hear a thing from him.

A week passed and Zombie never got back to me. Biff tried calling him. Nothing. We contacted his brother and he hadn't heard from or seen him either. I was extremely worried at that point. He wasn't even posting on social media. It was like he was gone.

Eventually, Biff heard from Zombie's twin. He said Zombie was okay and that he had told him to contact me. Zombie obviously didn't listen because my phone never rang or beeped. Another week passed and he still wasn't responding to me. I gave up after I had to eat Thanksgiving dinner alone.

The next weekend, I went to Biff's house. It was Friday night and we were just chilling on the couch watching TV. Biff decided she was going to call Zombie just to see if he would answer.

"He's not going to answer," I told her as I continued watching what was on the screen.

The phone rang a few times and then something crazy happened—he picked up.

"Something's been wrong with my phone," was his excuse.

Later that night, he came over to Biff's house. I let him give me some bullshit answer about his phone and how he couldn't contact me. I decided to give him a second chance. I told him he couldn't do that to me again. I was his girlfriend. We weren't just friends anymore. He couldn't just disappear for weeks and expect everything to be okay when he decided to show back up. He apologized profusely and said it wouldn't happen again. I told him if it did to not bother trying to speak to me because I would never give him another chance. We laid in bed that night and slept soundly.

Some time passed and everything was great. His communication was good, and we didn't have any issues. Christmas approached and he invited me to stay with him for the week. I agreed and we had a great time. He spent some time with my family, and we were able to spend a lot of time together. Time was hard to come by when we lived an hour apart.

The week ended and I needed to get back to Athens to work an overtime event. We decided our New Year's Eve plans would be separate; he wanted to spend time with his boys and I had made plans with Biff to attend a party at her house. Though our partying was going to be separate, we were going to end up back together at his house for the night.

Anyhoo, I drove back to Athens and had a work holiday party to go to that night. Zombie and I texted like usual, I went out, and I called him when I got back home. We talked for half an hour and then I went to sleep. The next day, I text him before I got to work. After I got done with the event, I realized I hadn't heard from him. I tried calling him while I drove home, but he didn't answer. Surely he wasn't doing this again . . . he was.

It was the night of the New Year's Eve party and I was supposed to be staying with Zombie. I hadn't heard from him, but I packed and gathered my things. I called Biff and told her what I was doing. I told her I was going to drop off the food I was bringing for the party and then I was going to go to Zombie's house. She said that was fine and if he didn't answer, I could stay at her place for the night.

An hour and a half later, I was at Biff's house. I unloaded my shit and my dog and went inside.

"Has he answered you yet?"

"No."

"Are you sure you want to go over there?"

"Yup. Positive. He can't ignore me if I'm on the front the porch."

"Okay, let me know what happens."

"Will do. Thanks for watching Queso." Queso is my dog, by the way. He's the cutest little Chihuahua ever.

Zombie only lived about ten minutes away from Biff, so it didn't take me long to get over there. When I got there, the house was dark. Zombie's car was gone and so was his brother's and his other roommate's. I decided to go knock on the door anyway, but of course, there was no answer. I called Zombie again and again. I was relentless. I was fucking pissed. He didn't pick up. Not once.

I called Biff and told her what happened. She told me to come on back, and without feeling a thing, I did. I went back to her house and got ready. Guests started showing up and the party was fun. We drank draanks and counted down with the TV at midnight. Things were okay for the moment. I would feel again tomorrow—that's what I told myself, and my plan was pretty successful until I pulled up Instagram. The first thing on my feed was a picture of Zombie with two girls from high school. His caption read "two GOATs" and he was clearly having a grand ole time.

I broke down. Biff took me into the bathroom and I cried like I had never cried before. I didn't stop crying for a month. I hoped and wished that I would hear from him. He answered the phone once, but I quickly found out that it happened by mistake. He was talking to some other people wherever he was at and clearly couldn't hear me calling out his name in his pocket.

It took some time, but I eventually got over it. Over it enough to stop crying and stop trying to contact him. Just when I decided to let go, he started poking at me. It's like they know. It's like fuckboys can read your mind. He started randomly liking my pictures on Instagram. He did that for months. I knew he was waiting for me to say something to him, but I never did. My friends and family—the same ones who told me to 'go for it' and 'you should give him a chance'—were now telling me to block him. I didn't do it. For some reason, I thought it was entertaining. I liked the idea that I was on his mind, but he wasn't getting any attention from me. It didn't bother me to see his face pop up in my notifications. It was something I laughed at.

About seven months had passed when it happened, when Zombie turned into just that—a zombie. He had disappeared like a ghost, but then he came back to life like nothing ever happened. I was on vacation with my family. I woke up and did what all millennials do, the young ones and the old ones, (shockingly, I'm still considered a millennial), and immediately picked up my phone. A few notifications popped up, and among them were a text message and a direct message on Instagram. I expected the text message to be from a guy I had been talking to. We had been texting the night before and I assumed he had fallen asleep because he hadn't responded before I went to bed myself.

When I opened my phone, I saw just how wrong I was. Staring up at me was Zombie's face.

"I miss you," the message said.

I shook my head and rubbed my eyes. I looked at the message again. "I miss you."

I closed out the thread and looked at my other notifications. The direct message on Instagram? It too was from Zombie. "I miss you."

The messages had been sent about half an hour apart, and both after 2:30 in the morning. Someone was clearly drunk and obviously missing him some Cole. Seeing those messages didn't bring me the feeling I thought I would have after hearing from him. Had he sent them seven months ago, maybe it would have been different. Maybe. But there we were.

My dad asked me what I was going to say. "Now's your chance to really lay into him," he said. "What are you going to do."

I looked at my dad and laughed. "I'm going to do exactly what he did to me. I'm not saying shit."

And I didn't, not for months. I eventually got curious enough to hear his excuse for what he did. He said—and I quote—"Remember when we were trying to be exclusive . . ."

I'm still stuck on that word *trying* because I'm pretty sure there was no trying. We were exclusive. WERE! Anyway, he went on to tell me that with the distance between us, he couldn't be exclusive and instead of being a grown-up and telling me, he just ghosted. He tried for months to get me to give him another chance, but I wouldn't budge. I had told him the first time he'd disappeared, I wasn't going to play the fool if he pulled that shit again and I'd meant it.

He eventually got a girlfriend but continued to try to hang out with me.

> **Me:** *Zombie, you have a girlfriend. Stop trying to talk to me. Go hang out with her.*
> **Him:** *You trippin.*

I'm trippin'? All the SMHing right here. Fuckboy to the fullest. And I'm the bitch?

EPISODE 16

THE DRIVER

*I*t was my twenty-something-or-other-th birthday weekend. Things were a little shaky with me and the guy I was "talking to" at the time, and I had no clue where things were going. I wanted him, and he wanted me, but not as much, or maybe he did, but it didn't matter because I was so far away and blah blah bleh—story of my life. I was attempting to get over him or not talk to him as much or both, so I wasn't going to include him in on my birthday plans. I wanted a girls' weekend anyway.

One of my good friends—we'll call her Leo—and I decided we were going to do our birthdays up that year and do fun stuff in Atlanta. Her birthday was in July and mine was in August, hence the name Leo (if you're into zodiac signs, then you'll know what I'm talking about). Which reminds me, that year was actually pretty big on the whole Leo thing. I'll go into that here. You know how I can get off on a tangent.

I listen to this very popular radio show. I'm not going to use its name because, one, I don't know if, by the time I release this book, that said radio show will still be on so you may not know what I'm talking about anyway, and two, because I don't want to get into the whole legal thing about name dropping, and three, you don't need to have ALL the details of my life, right?

Back to the original tangent . . .

I was a huge fan of that popular radio show (I still am if its still on) and it got a new host. Don't expect his name to be anywhere in this text. Anyway, he was hilarious, and using social media, I was able to see the face that went with the sexy voice on the radio, and let me tell you, that guy was a looker.

Well, I was extremely thirsty. Parched. I tried every which way I could think of to get that man to notice my existence. And he did. Eventually.

He was big on zodiac signs or, at least, on making fun of them. See, the guy was also a comedian and did videos every "season" making fun of whatever sign was up. I forget exactly what he said or how the fact that I'm a Leo came up, but he tweeted something and I tweeted a reply, not expecting anything back, but that man responded. Granted, he was making fun of me, but I had his attention and I was going to run with it, so it was all about Leos on Twitter for like a week that summer. I even got Leo (my friend, not the sign) to get on board with the whole thing and she tweeted up a storm too.

That kinda brings us back around to the original story-line here: Leo and I loved Leo season and loved our birth-days. And that year, we planned to do it up big.

For her birthday, we went to Atlanta to watch our Braves play. We, along with one of our other close girlfriends, had lots of drinks, lots of wings, and watched men throw around some balls. It was great.

A few weeks later, it was my birthday weekend and we planned another fun weekend in Atlanta. Leo and I were going to stay in a hotel in Buckhead and have a few drinks at the pool and then meet Biff at a restaurant before going out and partying the night away at some local bars.

When Friday came around, Leo and I both got off work a little early and made the drive down separately to the city. Once we both got to the hotel, it was time to get turnt! If you actually heard me say that, you'd crack up because it sounds extremely unnatural coming out of my mouth, which is one more reason why it's something I'd say.

After getting up to the room, which was completely outdated and kind of made me afraid to take my shoes off, and taking a shot or two, we changed into our bikinis and made our way down to the pool.

No one was down there when we arrived—an amazing, rare occurrence—but alas, it didn't last long. A mom and her two sons came down. Luckily, it was after Leo and I had taken our Snapchat selfies and pictures to add to our Instagram stories.

Leo stayed in the water, trying to get more photos, and I got out to lay in the chair and play on my phone. I didn't trust myself to hold my phone in the water. Not after the two shots and the large drink sitting next to me by the chair.

We hadn't been out there long when an older black man came out into the pool area. By the look of his uniform, he clearly worked for the hotel, but I wasn't quite sure in what capacity. He pulled a cigarette out of his pocket and lit it before taking a drag. (I don't smoke, so I'm not sure if that's the right or current terminology.)

He blew smoke out of his mouth and eyed Leo in the pool and then me, and then Leo again, and back over to me. I was waiting for him to say something. I knew it was coming.

He took another puff (again, I don't know if that's right—don't judge me) of his cigarette. "So, what brings you ladies to Atlanta?"

"Oh, we just celebrating her birthday," Leo answered from the pool.

She was cheesing so hard when she looked over at me. She knew I was trying not to crack up. I had to stifle the laughter. I took a sip of my drink and put my phone down in my lap. He started waddling over toward me. He stopped when he made it to the other side of my chair where he had a better view of both Leo and me.

"It's your birthday, huh?" he asked.

"It sure is." I smiled.

"So, how young are you turning?"

"Now, you know you're never supposed to ask a lady her age."

I actually don't know why this is a thing, or if it really is a thing anymore, but it sounded right to say to this guy. He was older, like maybe in his late fifties or early sixties, though because he was a black man, he might have been older because *black don't crack*. And in case you were wondering and didn't know already, I'm black. I figure I needed to clarify that at this point. Plus, if I got what I wanted, you can see my face right on the cover of this book, just so you can see for yourself.

Anyway, I'm pretty sure he's heard the phrase about asking a lady her age before and would drop it.

He chuckled. "You're right. What are y'all getting into tonight?" He looked back over to Leo in the water.

"Gonna grab some grub and then go out."

"Oooo. Where are y'all going to eat? Can I make some suggestions?"

"We have no idea. I'm trying to look up some places now," I said as I glanced up over my phone.

"Well, what kind of food do you like?" he asked.

"What kind of food do I *not* like is the real question."

Leo laughed. "Yeah, she been having a hard time trying to figure it out."

The man rubbed his belly and put out his cigarette. "Let me get in here and get you a birthday drink from the bar while y'all think about what kind of food you like." He started walking toward the door. "Do you at least know what kind of liquor you trying to sip on?" He laughed loudly, showing off, for the first time, his missing teeth.

"Uh . . . yeah . . . vodka, please!"

"You got it."

As soon as he got inside, Leo and I glared at each other and rolled our eyes. I'm surprised they didn't fall out the sides of our heads with how hard we rolled them.

"He better not be bringing me out a drink with drugs in it."

Leo craned her neck. "I can see him. He's at the bar. I'm watching."

Not long after, the man came back outside. He handed me a drink and I looked at Leo as I took it from his hands. She nodded, indicating to me the drink was okay.

"Thank you!"

"You're welcome."

"What is it?"

"Vodka cranberry."

"Oooo, yummy." I smiled and took a sip. It really was delicious.

"So, did y'all decide what kind of food you want?" he asked.

I looked over at Leo and realized she was talking on her phone. She looked at me out of the corner of her eye and quietly chuckled. She was leaving me alone on this one.

I picked up my phone and searched 'food near me'. A few

things popped up, but then I saw the place that was exactly where I didn't know I wanted to go: The Cheesecake Factory.

"Oooo! What about The Cheesecake Factory?" I looked over at Leo even though she was still on the phone.

She mumbled something into her phone and hung up. "What you say?"

"The Cheesecake Factory!"

"Cheesecake Factory?" The man chimed in and huffed. "I can make food better than that." He rubbed his belly and looked between us.

I looked at him momentarily before looking back at Leo with questioning eyes.

"Yeah, that sounds good to me. Text Biff and ask her if she's cool with it."

"So, what do y'all do anyway?" The guy asked, slipping his hands into his pocket and rocking back and forth.

"We have secret jobs. We can't tell you," Leo said.

"Secret jobs?" The man started waddling back to where he stood originally. "Y'all must be some strippers or something." He laughed loud, showing off his teeth, or lack thereof, again.

"You never know," I commented, smiling and shaking my head.

"Can you take a picture of us?" Leo asked, handing her phone out to the man.

He reached for it as I got up to join Leo back in the water. "Sure. Only if I can take one with you. You can send it to me."

"Why do you need to take one with us?" Leo asked as I waded through the water to get next to her.

"So I can show you ladies off. I can probably get other bitches by showing them a picture with two beautiful ladies like yourself."

Leo and I had no response. We just laughed and posed, hoping he would just take the picture and we could move on.

The man didn't say anything else and snapped a few shots for us. We both got out of the pool and started to towel off. I grabbed my phone and saw I had a text from Biff.

"She said Cheesecake Factory is cool," I told Leo. "And she's gonna just meet us here."

"All right."

Even though we were wrapped in our towels and putting our shoes on, the man asked us where we were going.

"We're going upstairs to get ready," I said.

"Well, I'll tell you what. Since it's your birthday, I can give y'all a ride to Cheesecake Factory."

Leo and I looked at each other and then back at the man.

"Y'all see that limo parked up front?" he asked.

"No," Leo said.

"Well, there's a limo owned by the hotel. I'm the driver. I can take y'all to dinner. Just come find me after you get ready."

"Sure thing," I said as I grabbed Leo's arm, pulling her to the door.

So I'm sure you thought this story was all about that old man with no teeth since the episode is called The Driver. I'm sorry to burst your bubble, but this story is not about the creepy man at the hotel.

We got ready. Biff met us in our room. We drank more drinks, went downstairs, and avoided the man like the plague while we waited for our Uber. This story isn't about that driver either.

The story really begins after we ate at The Cheesecake Factory, which was delicious by the way, even though I had a bad taste in my mouth after some lady and I almost got into a fist fight after she tried to cut us in line and then run her mouth. You don't cut in line at The Cheesecake Factory. Oh no. You're not about to turn my hour wait into an hour and a half.

Anyway, I promised you a driver. This episode is about our second Uber driver, the one who picked us up from dinner and drove us to the bars.

On the way to dinner, I took one for the team and sat up front with the first Uber driver. When the after-dinner Uber pulled around the corner, I ran to the back door. It was someone else's turn to take the awkward seat. Biff decided to be the champion that time, but as Leo and I were opening the back doors, we noticed how attractive our driver looked.

"You should sit up front," Leo mouthed to me as we started getting in the back.

I shrugged my shoulders. Too late now. It would be too awkward to move.

"How you ladies doing?" The Driver asked as we all shut our doors.

"Good!" we said in unison.

"We're just heading out for this one's birthday!" Leo exclaimed.

"Oh, really?" he asked.

That's when I noticed it. He had an accent.

"Are you from the islands?" I asked.

"Yeah, I'm from the Bahamas. Can you tell?"

"I thought I heard an accent." I blushed. He couldn't see me though because I was behind him, so I guess it didn't matter.

"Hole in the Wall, huh?" he asked, referring to the bar we were headed to.

"Yeah. Have you been?"

"Yeah, it's pretty cool. You should have fun there."

"So, do you drive all night?" I asked.

"No. I usually drive til about 11 and then I take off to go out or whatever."

"You should come out with us!"

"Oh, really?"

"Yeah," I said as we pulled up to the bar. "Give me your number and I'll let you know if we move bars before 11."

The Driver laughed and shook his head but called out his number. I typed it into my phone and thanked him for the ride. Biff, Leo, and I all hopped out and went into the bar.

We stayed inside Hole in the Wall for a while. It was fun. There were two bars, pool tables, and great music. It was a wonderful atmosphere, and it didn't hurt that the bartender gave us a couple rounds of free shots, which made it harder for me to complain when I ordered a vodka tonic and he told me it was twelve dollars. Now, mind you, I'm used to going to bars in Athens. In Athens, a vodka tonic is like five bucks.

"Twelve dollars."

"Excuse me?" I yelled over the music.

"Twelve!"

"Well, okay." I pulled out my cash and paid, but didn't order another drink at the bar.

It wasn't long after that when I pulled out my phone and sent a text to the number The Driver had given me. I asked him if he was coming out, and a few minutes later he told me he was already in the bar waiting for me to text him. He said he looked for us, but he couldn't find us. I asked him where he was and he told me he was at the bar by the door, which was the one opposite of where we were.

I grabbed the girls, and we walked over to the other bar. I hadn't really seen The Driver full on from the back of the car, but I recognized the hat and the little sideways grin he gave me when he saw me. There were a few other women around him, but he scooted his way out of the bunch and walked toward me, Leo, and Biff.

When we reached him, I gave him a hug like I'd known

the guy for years, not like I had just met him hours prior. He was a good hugger.

"You made it!" I yelled over the music.

"Yeah, of course! It's your birthday."

"Let me get some of that," I said as I reached out for the Black and Mild in his fingers.

He started to hand it to me, but I stopped him before I took it. "Wait. Is this really a Black and Mild?" I asked.

"Yes?" he said, confused. "What else would it be?"

"I was tricked once. When I was in college, my friends thought it would be funny if they tricked me into smoking weed. I never wanted to smoke weed—it just wasn't my thing —but I liked Black and Milds. So, one night when I was drunk they handed me what I thought was a Black and Mild and didn't tell me that it was actually weed until the next morning. I was pissed."

He laughed. "Nah, it's really a Black and Mild."

I took the small cigar from him and had a little.

"You see those girls?" he asked as I handed his cigar back to him.

"Yeah, the ones you were standing with?"

"Uh huh. They wanted to go to Edgewood." He cocked his head back and started laughing.

"What you mean?" I asked.

"I was driving and they wanted to go to Edgewood, but I convinced them to come here because I didn't want to drive to Edgewood and back. I told them Buckhead would be more fun."

"You made them come here knowing you were coming to meet me?" I was appalled . . . and slightly flattered.

"Yeah. They'll be all right. I bought them drinks."

"I was wondering why they were giving us the stink eye." I smacked him on his arm and laughed.

The rest of the night was pretty chill. We drank, danced,

and talked. My friends and I eventually moved on to another bar later that night and then went back to the room to hang out and chill. We left The Driver at the first bar, but apparently I texted him and invited him to come to the room. He declined, being a gentleman, and he joked with me about the invitation in our conversations over the next few months.

* * *

A FEW WEEKS after our first encounter, Driver wanted to take me out on a date. I hadn't been on a real first date in I couldn't remember how long, so I was pretty excited. Somehow, I had managed to pull two dates that weekend.

The first was with a guy I met on one of the various dating sites. I'm pretty sure it was Hinge. He planned a date at an escape room, and I have to give him credit for originality. The escape room was pretty fun, but we lost so that sucked because I'm pretty competitive, and I just knew he wasn't it as soon as he said hello. I was already iffy on him, but then I heard his voice and I just couldn't. Maybe that was me being picky, or maybe it was just me knowing what I like. I went on with the date and even beyond his voice, it just wasn't going to work. We weren't compatible.

Anyway, the second date that weekend was with Driver. We made plans for Sunday, and he offered to drive to Athens to meet me. I thought that was sweet because it was a little over an hour from his place. He never mentioned anything about staying the night, so driving a total of two hours to just go to dinner with me? He was already making the right moves.

We met at one of the local breweries. This brewery was closer to the highway than other ones in town and I actually hadn't been to that one yet. It hadn't been in Athens for long, so I was pretty excited to try it. I was a little bit nervous because I kind of liked this guy. We had been communicating frequently since we'd met, but I didn't really *know him*, know him. I had also kind of forgotten what he looked like. I remember thinking he was cute, but let's be honest, it was dark and I was drunk. I had texted Leo and Biff about it and Biff said she couldn't remember what he looked like and Leo said she remembered him being cute, but he may have had big gums. We all know how I am about teeth, so it was going to be interesting.

I walked in a few minutes late, and Driver was sitting at the bar. A couple sitting near him said something to him while they were looking at me. He turned around with a huge smile on his face. He was cuter than I remembered, and his gums—they weren't *that* big.

I sat down at the bar between him and the couple. He was already sipping on a beer. I ordered a flight and we ordered food and that was that. It was simple. Conversation was easy and we got along great, even without having consumed a lot of liquor. I really enjoyed his company.

We spent a few hours there, and after the date, he walked me to my car. We spent a little while longer talking and eventually, he leaned in for a kiss. It was nice and sweet and I let him kiss me again before I got in my car. He watched me pull out of the lot and we went our separate ways.

The following week, Driver asked me if he could take me on another date. I told him I would love that. He again offered to drive to Athens and of course, I had no problem with that. The less I had to drive, the better. He told me to make a plan and he'd meet me wherever. I decided it was okay for him to meet me at my house and then we could Uber to dinner. It was large pitcher special night at my favorite Mexican restaurant in town, so I knew we'd be doing that. And the way that restaurant made their pitchers, neither one of us would be able to drive.

When he arrived, I ordered the Uber, and in no time, one showed up. We got dropped off at the restaurant. Driver earned extra points when he asked me if I wanted to order a large cheese dip. However, he lost points when he stuck his chip in the dip, sucked the cheese off of the chip, and then stuck said chip back into the queso. I was baffled and confused and hurt that he would treat the cheese dip that way.

"Why'd you do that?" I couldn't help myself. I had to ask.

He shrugged his shoulders. "I like the cheese. I don't like the chip."

Blasphemy.

I decided to shrug it off. I mean, at least the man liked cheese. You may be shocked to know, I've dated some guys who don't.

Extreme blasphemy.

After the crazy queso fiasco, things were all fine and dandy. The date, again, was going great. Then he started video chatting with some of his friends from the Bahamas. They were at some party and the video was loud. The music was loud. Their talking was loud. Driver was loud. And we were sitting down to dinner in a restaurant! My favorite restaurant, by the way. A restaurant where the hosts and hostesses, waiters and waitresses recognize me, and here I am with someone who doesn't understand table manners. Queso and phone call manners! I was embarrassed and I was ready to go.

We finished up our food and grabbed another Uber. I decided to play it safe and take him to one of the bars downtown. There was no cheese dip and you could be as loud as you wanted. Once we got to the bar, Driver bought us some drinks and we chilled. The rest of the date was great, and I remembered why I liked him.

The two of us hung out with each other and together

with our friends for a little over a month. Things were never made official, but it seemed like they were headed that way. The last night we hung out before things changed was at Biff's.

A group of us hung out and then there was talk of the two of us possibly getting together the following day. I was headed to Athens later in the evening because I had to go visit my family for my little brother's birthday, but Driver talked about possibly coming to take me to dinner when I got back.

Him: Hola

Him: You went back home yet

Me: No, I'm still at pop's house for my brother's bday

Him: Happy bday, Bro

Me: I'll tell him!

Me: You still tryna come see me?

Him: Not today. Got some stuff I'm trying to deal with at the moment. Sorry, I would've loved to.

Me: Everything all right?

Him: No

Him: But I'm good

Him: Thanks for asking

Me: [sad emoji]

Me: Hope everything gets better

I didn't hear from him at all on Monday. Tuesday night my phone dinged.

Him: Hey

Him: Sup

Me: Hey there

Him: Wyd

Me: Setting up my laptop finally.

Him: O ok
Him: Well I gotta go home for a couple of weeks
Me: Like Bahamas?
Him: Yes
Me: When? How come?
Him: Family business
Me: When do you have to leave?
Him: Early morning
Me: [two crying emojis]
Him: I'll call u in an hour

He never called me. I figured he may have gotten busy and forgotten or didn't have time to give me a call before his flight. In today's day and age, it didn't seem plausible, but I figured I'd give him the benefit of the doubt. He was only going to be gone for two weeks, right?

Wrong.

Two weeks came and went and not a peep. I tried texting him to make sure everything was okay and got no response. I started off worried and then, after remembering all of the shit I went through with Zombie, I got mad. I got fucking ghosted again. A-fucking-gain. I threw my hands in the air and gave up.

Fast forward two months after the 'I'll call u in an hour' text and some rando messages me 'hey' on Insta. So, you know on Insta how the profile picture is, like, super tiny? Yeah, the picture was so small, it really took some investigative work for me to figure out that it wasn't a rando at all. It was Driver.

I wasn't initially receptive to Driver, but eventually, I decided to hear him out. He didn't quite tell me why he had to leave for the Bahamas in the first place or how two weeks turned into two months, but I got the impression it had something to do with his citizenship status.

It didn't take long for him to hook me again. Our conversations had always been great, and the time apart didn't change that. He was living with some family in Florida now, so seeing each other wasn't something that could happen as easily as it had before.

One night we had been talking on the phone about just that. Driver said something along the lines of 'but what if we could see each other?'. He tried to video chat me not long after that, but something was going on with our phones and we couldn't get the video to connect. The audio was working, but I couldn't see him. We both hung up and a few seconds later, he sent me a message telling me to hold on. So, I did. I held on for three days. I finally texted him and told him I was done. I didn't have time for the games and I was tired of getting disappeared on. It had happened to me before and he had already done it twice. I was good.

He never responded that night, but the next night, I got a call.

"Please let me explain."

"Why should I?"

"I know . . . I don't deserve it, but please? Let me at least explain what happened."

"Fine."

"Well, you know how that night I said something about being able to see you?"

"Yeah."

"I was in Atlanta."

"What?!"

"Yeah, I was in Atlanta and I was going to come surprise you. My homeboy needed me to drop something off for him. So, the plan was for me to drop the thing off and then come and surprise you in Athens, but my friend wanted to grab a drink. I didn't think it would be a bad idea to grab one, but I should have just driven to you."

"What happened?" I was curious to know, but I had a lot of other emotions running through my head. I was mad that something had kept him from coming to see me. I was excited that he had tried to come see me. Most of all though, I was a little apprehensive, freaked out, and confused as to why he thought he could just show up at my house.

"We went to get a drink and afterward, in the parking lot, we got into an argument with some guys. One thing led to another and we started fighting for real. The cops showed up and I got arrested. That's why I haven't contacted you. I've been in jail."

Uuuuh? What the hell was I supposed to do with that?

Things were never quite the same after that. I tried to let it go but I couldn't. He didn't understand why it was a bad idea.

"He came after me. What was I supposed to do? Run away?"

"That would have been an option to keep you out of jail, yeah."

We talked about me going to visit him in Florida, but things were just weird. He was introducing me to his family over video chats and they were telling me things like 'make sure you treat our boy right' and 'I've heard wonderful things about you' and ish like that. I wasn't comfortable with it. We weren't there yet, but what was I supposed to do? Be rude to his dad? That was not an option.

I looked at flights to go see him, but then my gut told me not to do it. I tried to express my feelings to him, but he just wasn't getting it. He kept looking at flights and sending me prices and I knew I had to break it off. We talked a few times on the phone and I tried to end it in the nicest way possible, but either he didn't understand or he was ignoring the message I tried to relay.

Thursday
Me: Hey... I don't think I can come
Him: Ok
Saturday
Him: You upset
Me: Nah, just been busy
Him: Tru
Sunday
Him: So it's like that between us now... Just asking
Me: Like what?
Him: Hey. It's nothing
Him: How are you
Me: Can't complain. Tired.
Him: Wyd
Me: Chores
Him: Always on top of it ......
Me: What's with the dots
Him: Well I'm about to go into the Lord's house, but I just wanted to say that I'm sorry if I made you feel any way of me
Me: What do you mean?
Him: I'm just saying the way we communicate changed being busy an' all. Don't return my missed calls, short answer text, etc..... I don't want it to seem like I'm in 'love' or anything, but I thought different of you/us that's all.
Him: Maybe it was the travel/talking to my family, but like I said it wasn't serious and all my friends are family literally.
Me: I mean, it's just a lot. It seems like we're both busy, you live far away now, you've made it clear you're not moving back this way . .

.

Side note: This man at one point told me he wouldn't move back to Georgia unless he had a reason to move back to Georgia and then smiled at me super hard.

. . . and I can't date someone who lives in another state... It also just seems like you want certain things that I'm not willing to give you right now, and I've got my own issues with trust and feeling a certain way and I know that's not ALL on you and it's not fair and I'm trying to work on it, but I can't tell you when that will happen. And I really do have a lot on my plate right now
Him: *That's just it, what your* saying is the complete opposite.*

*can we please talk about how I hate when someone can't use the correct form of you're in text?

Me: *What I'm saying? Opposite of what?*
Him: *Everything*
Him: *Can u call me? This texting is confusing**

*Every time the two of us texted about something, if he didn't like the way it was going, he would all of a sudden become confused and not understand written English.

Me: *I will before I go to bed*

If he wanted it loud and clear and concise so he could understand we. were. not. going. to. work, then that's what he'd get.

I called him that night, and after getting ghosted on twice, bad communication, and rushed relationshipy things, I had had enough. The early great conversations and initial attraction didn't matter anymore. Once we got on the phone, I broke it down for him. We weren't going to work. He, in turn, tried to turn the entire thing around on me and tried to act like I had made the whole thing up. Like I had just imagined how into me he was and how he just wanted to be friends. Oooh, yeah, there's more.

"Before you go, can I ask you something and you not get mad at me?" he asked.

"I can't answer that question honestly."

"Why not?"

"I don't know the question, so I don't know if I'm going to get mad or not, but I have a feeling if you're asking me not to get mad at you, then I'm going to get mad."

"Well, can you promise me you won't get mad."

"No, Driver. Just ask me the damn question or don't."

"Okay. Well, you know how you don't like to share your feelings?"

"Sure . . ." *Not true, I just didn't care to share my feelings with him.*

"Do you think you drink a lot to cover them up, so you don't have to share?" he asked in all seriousness.

"Excuse me?" I was seething.

"Do you think you drink a lot s—"

I cut him off right there. "Are you accusing me of being an alcoholic?"

"No. I'm just sayi—"

"You? Seriously? You're asking me that, when every fucking time you call me—in the middle of the week, mind you—you're drunk. And some of the time, you don't even remember talking to me even though you called me? You? That person is asking me if I drink excessively??"

"Oh. We're not going to go ther—"

"And speaking of not sharing things. You still haven't told me why the fuck you disappeared for two months!"

"You're still on that?" And then Driver laughed a laugh I will never forget.

I saw black, and before I said something I was going to regret, I hung up. I felt a rush of relief wash over me. If that wasn't clear enough that we were done, I couldn't help the man.

He immediately called me back, but I didn't answer. He called again. No answer. He sent me a text.

Him: *What was that? Did u hang up on me?*

No response. I was too busy blocking him on Instagram.

Him: *Fyi how rude.*

Block. And y'all know I don't block people.

EPISODE 17

THE ATHLETE

*W*hat was I thinking? I wish I could tell you. I should have known better. You see a pattern here, don't you? I haven't been the brightest when it comes to making men decisions. Mencisions.

Even at twenty-seven, I'm still making the same mistakes. But I swear, it's not all me. It's them too. I don't know what is in the waters these days, but men are awful. At least, all of the ones I have even been slightly romantically or sexually involved with.

I should have known.

I was in college once, as you learned from the early episodes of my truth. When I was in college, athletes were not good. And I don't mean their athletic ability or as human beings; I'm talking about as a boyfriend or anything remotely close to that type of a relationship.

You wanted a hook-up? You wanted to be a booty call? You wanted to be the side piece or the main chick knowing there were side pieces? You wanted the occasional different dick while you had your own thing going on? Athletes were your go-to.

I could have had many an athlete while I was in college, but as you know, my head was stuck far up someone else's ass. For this reason, I kept them at arm's length and got my flirt on. That was the extent of my interaction with the college football and basketball players. I didn't want any of the above-listed items, so what was the point?

At twenty-seven, why did I think that they would be any different? I'm grown, okay. Not the 'I'm a legal adult, so I'm grown, mom and dad' grown. I'm grown as fuck. #Adulting-Sucks grown. Yet, I still fell under the spell.

Once my head wasn't lost in someone's rear end, and I was free to do what I pleased, I could do more than flirt with the athlete. But I wanted a relationship, right? So, it wasn't the fact that he was an athlete that drew me to him.

It was the fact that he said I was beautiful and he was friends with my friend and my friend said he was sweet and nice. And it's really only sweet and nice guys who call you beautiful and not sexy or get your attention with the 'aye, girl' . . . right?

He was only twenty-one and he was still in college and he was an athlete. No big deal. Right?

Let me tell you why I was so so wrong . . . again.

I was working an event. And no, I'm still not going to tell you what it is I did for a living. It's a tiny detail that isn't that important, so . . . anyhoo . . .

I was working a part time at a basketball season opener. It was a double header. Women played first and men were on second. I got there early for pre-game stuff and my position was down on the floor. I was looking for the chair that was supposed to be in my spot when the men's team was coming off the floor, so that the women could come on and practice.

A few of them walked past me, while a small group of them huddled up together looking in my direction. That's when he caught my eye. He was staring at me with beautiful chocolate brown eyes and a smile on his face that had to be one of the most gorgeous smiles I'd ever seen. I could feel myself blushing. Trying to remain as professional as possible, I quickly looked away.

Unable to help myself, I looked back and the group was making its way through the small space past me. He was still looking. I was about to look away again when he said, "Oh, my God. You're beautiful."

It took a second for what he'd said to register, and for me to realize he was actually talking to me. I choked out a 'thank you' and heard some of the guys kinda snicker. Another one said 'I knew it. I knew you were gonna think she looked good when I saw her.' A grin grew large on my face.

The women's team eventually got on the floor and I found my seat. After I sat down, I texted my girlfriends in our group message and told them about the athlete who'd said I was beautiful. That's when one of my girls said he was her homie and she would have to text him for me.

To be honest, I didn't think anything of my friend texting him and took it with a grain of salt. I was sure it was going to go nowhere. I just enjoyed the view as he played, once the men finally had their time on the court. He was just as sexy on the court as he had been when he walked past me with that sexy, smug look on his face. He was so sweaty and there is just something about the smell of a man playing a sport that gets me . . . I need to stop, or I am going to be writing an entirely different genre of story here.

After the game, I didn't give the interaction too much thought. A couple days passed before my friend mentioned him again. She said she had spoken to him about me and he'd said he wanted my Instagram handle. She asked me if it was cool and I told her to go for it. Eventually, she gave me his number. I wasn't going to text him right away. Gotta play the game.

A while later in the day, I had an Instagram notification telling me he had added me. I followed him back and shortly after realized he'd unfollowed me. That was clue number one. Which, of course, I completely ignored.

Unphased, I liked one of his pictures. Seconds later, the following thread unfolded:

Him: You playing the liking game
Me: Haha, nah, I'm not playing a game lol
Him: What you call it then?
Me: Liking something I'm looking at
Him: Lol what you like
Me: That smile is pretty nice I guess [smirk emoji]
Him: [small smile emoji] seen me checking you out?
Me: I may have caught on to that haha
Him: [his number]

Even though I already had his number from my friend, since he sent it to me, I figured I'd go ahead and shoot him a text. I let him know I saved his number and we chit-chatted briefly until we both passed out asleep.

Little flirty messages continued over the next week. I could really see why my friend said he was sweet. He seemed like a genuinely nice guy and I was enjoying talking to him and getting to know him. When his name popped up on my screen, I automatically smiled. I felt like a girl with a kinder-garten crush.

There was one night he was flying back into town from an out-of-state basketball game. It was late as hell and I couldn't believe the team was coming back that night.

Me: It's gonna be late AF lol when do you sleep??
Him: I don't sleep. I'm coming to sleep with you.
Me: How you gonna come sleep with me when you don't sleep?

Him: Lol I might be able to fall asleep with you
Me: Lol oh you think so huh?
Him: Lol yeah [two crying laughing emojis]
Me: Smh I mean my bed really is the most comfortable. I be passing out real quick. Haha
Him: Lol invite me
Me: Haha it ain't that easy. It's gonna take more than that to get in my bed. [sexy smirking emoji]
Him: Ain't nun wrong with that

Nice guy, right? I thought so. He didn't push it any further. Didn't ask again about coming over and seemed to respect my wishes.

We continued texting back and forth throughout the week, and he was playing in a home basketball game a few days later. I actually didn't have to work the game, so I talked with my girlfriends and we decided we would all go to cheer on him and the rest of the team. I told him I was going to watch him play, and he seemed pretty stoked at the idea.

That night, I met my friend with her adorable little son, Aiden, at the venue. We got some snacks and found a seat. It was already the second half and our team was up, but it was close. I looked down on the floor where the men's team was huddled up in a timeout and I spotted him. His chocolate skin glistened with sweat and the focus on his face turned me on instantly. Then I noticed how hard he was smacking on a piece of gum.

I turned to say something to my friend about it and before I could open my mouth, she looked at me, cracking up, and said, "Why the hell is he chewing on that gum like that?"

I started laughing too and told her I was about to say the same damn thing.

Before the game ended, our other friend joined us and we

all sat enjoying what was left of the game. Our team won and he was definitely something to look at. He was a great player and a beautiful specimen.

My girlfriends told me to make sure I let him know I was there and to keep them posted. We all parted ways, and when I finally made it back home, I sent him a text letting him know I had been able to watch him play, and told him it was a great game.

He responded quicker than I thought he would.

> *Him: Thank you*
> *Me: What you getting into tonight?*
> *Him: I don't even know what it is to do*
> *Me: Have a couple drinks*
> *Him: I might*
> *Me: You should do it with me*
> *Him: Ima want to fuck soo and ion know how you feel about that*

I should have just left it alone at this point. I shouldn't have responded so quickly. Hindsight tells me I should have just let that simmer for a minute before I continued with the flirting. I liked that man. We got along and I wanted to get to know him better and he really did seem like a sweet, nice guy. But . . . he was sexy and I was very attracted to him and I wanted to have sex and I have no problem admitting that I am a grown woman who likes to get the D. And the fact that he was sweet and nice and hadn't pushed me into sleeping with him before made me want to fuck him so much more in that moment.

> *Me: Haha I mean . . . I definitely want to, but there's a couple reasons why I shouldn't tonight*
> *Him: Why is that?*

*Me: Well one, my wax appointment isn't until the morning lol and
the other reason is I'm trying real hard not to be that girl*

Reason One: Y'all don't understand—that shit was bad. I
had recently started getting Brazilian waxes. For those of you
who don't know what that is, it's when someone spreads hot
wax all over your pussy and between your ass cheeks and
then yanks out all of the hair attached to it. It's beautiful
afterward and smooth as a baby's bottom. And, in the words
of one of my very best friends, you'll be in the shower afterward and feel how soft it is and you'll look down and say 'oh?
That's me?' Also, don't ever believe your friend if she tells
you 'it doesn't hurt that bad'. I have a high tolerance for pain
and that shit is terrible. I almost punched the woman who
ripped off the first strip. It was a reflex, but I caught myself.
But it's totally worth it, I swear. I still get it done. Beauty is
pain, right?

Anyway, it had been six weeks since I'd had my last wax,
so it was extra fuzzy down there. To each his own, but I like
my shit buck naked. I had made an appointment for the
following morning for that very reason. And by that I mean,
I'd had a feeling I was going to be hanging out with The
Athlete that Friday night and wanted a reason *not* to fuck
him. I didn't want to be sporting a bush the first time we
hooked up.

Reason Two: I had decided I didn't want to hook up with
a guy the first time I hung out with him. I wanted to at least
give it a couple times. Try something different. Switch up my
pattern.

About an hour later and two Winter Jack ciders in, and
my two reasons were beyond me. I texted him again.

*Me: But I definitely want to... and get enough liquor in me [eyes up
at ceiling emoji]*

I didn't hear from him for a couple of hours. I had another Winter Jack cider and I'm not sponsored by Jack Daniel's Whiskey or anything, but y'all. Winter Jack is my jam. It's cinnamony and warm and with just enough alcohol in it to make you feel all cozy. I was lying in bed when I noticed my phone was lit up. The Athlete was calling me. I answered on what had to have been the last ring because as soon as I said hello, there was silence and then he hung up. I looked down at my phone and saw that I had received two back-to-back messages from him.

> **Him:** *I want to*
> **Him:** *You playing*
> **Me:** *I answered*
> **Me:** *You hung up*
> **Him:** *What you doing*

Mind you, it was now after 1 am ... booty call ... yeah ... I told y'all from the beginning I should have known better.

> **Me:** *Laying in the bed. Debating another drink.*
> **Him:** *Need to come lay with me*

An hour and fifteen minutes later, I was picking the man up from his place. I had parked in a spot and he told me he was standing at the curb a little further down. I started pulling closer to him and even in the dark, he looked good. He was in his athletic sweats and was carrying a backpack over his shoulder and a duffel bag in his hand. The team was going out of the country for a week, and I had agreed to drop him off where he needed to be the next morning.

He opened up my back door and tossed his bags in.

"What's up?" he asked as he hopped in the front passenger seat.

"Not much. How's it going?"

"Good."

We kinda stared at each other briefly. It was the first time we had been in such close proximity. We eyed one another as if to measure if we were as attracted to each other up close as we had been on the basketball court and through our phones.

"You want your seat warmer on. It's kinda cold outside. My car's fancy like that." I get a little awkward when I'm around someone I like for the first time.

"I see that. Ima have to drive it some time."

"Oh, really?"

"Yeah. You gonna let me."

Direct. I liked it.

After we made the short trip back to my house, I walked him through the back door and upstairs to the kitchen.

"This is nice," he remarked as he looked around at my home.

"Thanks. Do you want a drink?" I asked as I finally settled on that third glass of cider.

"Nah. I'm good."

"You sure? You don't want water or anything?"

"No thanks." He plopped down on my couch.

Now I was all for chilling and hanging out and everything. That's what I had wanted to do earlier in the night, but we were approaching three in the morning. Normally, that wouldn't be an issue, but seeing as how we had to be up by seven so I could get him where he needed to be, chilling wasn't really on the agenda anymore . . . not when there was sex to be had.

"So . . . you want to chill down here or go up to the room?" I asked.

He didn't even say a word. With a smile on his face, he stood up really quick and followed me up the stairs. Before I even had my dog put away and the door shut behind me, his shirt was already off, and he was climbing into my bed. Somehow, he already knew which side of the bed to lay on. I actually just thought of that now as I was writing it.

Anyway, I crawled into the bed after him—into *my* side of the bed—and swallowed a gulp of my cider. I tried to make small talk, having developed the jitters for what was about to happen. He took one of his huge hands and slapped the inside of my sweatpants covered thigh. I quickly took another sip of my drink. He slapped the inside of my thigh again and began rubbing my leg softly and slowly. I downed what was left in my cup and tossed it onto the floor. I began taking my pants off, wanting to feel his hands on my bare skin. He ripped off the rest of his clothes and in record time, we were both naked.

He kissed me and then traced his tongue around the different lines of my ears and the curve of my neck. It felt so amazing. He climbed on top of me and you know what happened next, folks.

I clearly forgot about my hairy vagina and resolving to see a guy more than once before hooking up. I didn't think about anything other than the fact that he fit inside of me like a hot dog inside a bun. Like cheese on mac. Like whiskey and ginger ale.

He woke me up a couple hours later with his hand on my breast for round two. An hour after that, I woke him up with my lips on his dick for round three. So much for sleep, right?

After the third time was done, he got up out of bed and went into the restroom to clean himself up. I laid in the bed and closed my eyes for the few moments I had left and waited for him to finish so I could use the bathroom for the same thing.

A little before seven, I was putting on my shoes and asked if he was ready.

"Yup."

"All right. Let's go."

I smiled at him as he stood up from my bed and he smiled back. However, there was something there—a look that didn't quite go with the smile. Another clue.

We got in the car and started driving to the gym where I needed to drop him off. I made a turn and he said something that sounded like 'you could have . . .' and then some mumbling.

"What?" I asked him as I turned to look at him.

He shook his head. "Nothing." The word was barely audible.

"You saying I could have kept going straight?"

"Yeah, you could have."

I smirked. "I know."

I looked over at him and he was looking out the window. Had I said something wrong? Something was definitely off about his demeanor, but I wasn't quite sure what. I'll never know the answer.

Most of the car ride was quiet. We got closer to the gym and I finally filled the silence.

"I'm gonna be tired as fuck all day." I smiled, thinking about why that was going to be.

"What time do you have to be at work?" His voice was different now than it had been seconds prior. More chipper. Happier. Speaking like he actually wanted to talk to me.

"I don't have to be there until one."

"Man, you got all day to sleep." He chuckled.

"I got shit to do." I laughed.

He didn't say anything in response.

I pulled up to the curb to drop him off and the car rolled to a stop. He opened the car door and hopped out.

"Let me get this other bag out the back seat."

He shut the front door and opened the back, grabbing his bag. "Thanks for dropping me off. I'll text you later."

"Sounds good," I called after him.

We smiled at each other and he shut the door. I pulled away and made my way back home.

When I got back into my room, I noticed a shirt that wasn't mine laid across the back of the chair under the window. I picked it up and immediately got a whiff of the best smelling cologne, or body wash, or laundry detergent, or mixture of the three that I had ever had the pleasure of smelling before. Cinnamon, clove, man. My nose was very grateful.

I tossed the shirt back on the chair and hopped in the shower. I ran my errands and made it back to my house. After sleeping for a little bit, I finally got up to get ready for work. My eyes found the shirt on the chair again.

(11:52 am)
Me: You left your shirt over here

Radio silence. All day. But he was traveling. Not a big deal.

(9:02 pm)
Me: Hope you had a good trip and a good day

After a long day and essentially no sleep the night before, I passed out under the covers. I didn't look at my phone again until the next morning. There was no response.

The team had gone out of the country for a game. The schedule showed a game on Monday and they had flown out on a Saturday morning. It was now Sunday and I hadn't heard from him. It wouldn't have been so weird, since he wasn't my boyfriend or anything, except for the fact that ever since we had started communicating, we had talked every day.

Maybe he couldn't text from where he was? Maybe he was busy with practice? Maybe this or maybe that? I didn't know.

I laid in my bed and started looking at people's Instagram stories and Snapchat stories. It only took a few scrolls to realize he had posted stories on both. Yesterday. Before and after both of my texts to him. I shrugged my shoulders and hopped out of the bed and went on about my day.

Later that night, I was on social media again and noticed more posts from him. I decided to comment on one of the things he'd posted on Snap and saw later he had opened the message but didn't respond. I sent him a second message and told him to let me know when he wanted his shirt back. Not long after, I got the notification telling me he was typing back. Shocker. I opened the message once he finished typing.

"You can just throw it away."

I immediately looked away from my phone and did a double take. Looking back at the screen seconds later, I reread the message.

"You can just throw it away."

Funny thing about any type of written message is you can't really know how things are being said. I didn't know how to take the message. Was he just saying he didn't care about the shirt, so I could throw it away? Or was it more of, I don't plan on seeing you again, so throw that shit away? After being ignored for a few messages, I was leaning toward the second, but he was a nice, sweet guy. Surely it was how I first perceived it.

I messaged back something along the lines of 'huh?'. He opened that message and didn't respond.

Days went by and I came to realize the team was playing in a tournament that essentially lasted the entire week. He continued posting shit on social media and viewing the things I posted, but I didn't hear a peep.

I met with our mutual friend the following Friday to go shopping. There were Black Friday deals going on. If you didn't already think I was crazy, I'm sure finding out my friend and I were attempting to brave the Mall of Georgia on Black Friday, you'd find me a little nuts after all.

On the ride over, my girlfriend mentioned how The Athlete had texted her the night before saying they had just touched down and asking about a Thanksgiving dinner plate. She had been updated on what was going on with us, and she told me to text him a simple hello since the team was back in town.

(2:36 pm)
Me: Hey you

My friend and I spent the next few hours getting some shopping done. Finding a parking spot was actually the most difficult part of the whole trip. Inside, the mall wasn't as packed as I thought it would be. A couple of stores were super hot, but all in all, it wasn't a terrible trip. And I got some nice gifts for my family.

We got back in the car and I realized I hadn't heard back from him. My friend looked to see if he had posted anything during the day.

"I know that boy has been on his phone today," she said as she started scrolling through Instagram.

"I can probably look and see if he was on today." I was looking through my own phone. That's one of the great things about Insta if you want to social media stalk. You can't tell on people's actual pages, but if you have a message thread with them, it will tell you when they were active.

"He's on right now," I told her.

"Is he?" she asked.

I turned my phone to face her and showed her the little green dot next to his name.

She shook her head. "I don't know why he's acting like that."

"Should I say something to him?"

"Yeah, girl. It's been all day. He could say something." My friend continued shaking her head.

She knew him better than I did, so if she said it would be okay to send him another message, then I was going to send him another message. I didn't want to be annoying, but I felt like after a week of silence, I deserved some sort of an answer. We had gotten along great and I thought the sex was good. It wasn't awkward at all, not even the first time, and trust me, he definitely was satisfied every single time.

My friend started driving, and together we constructed the perfect message.

Me: Hey, look I noticed you ain't really been answering, so you can let me know if you aren't interested or whatever. I was cool with being friends and getting to know each other, but if you ain't about it, that's cool, just let me know . . .

Made it home. No response.

Woke up at two in the morning with a stomach virus. No response.

Spent an entire day throwing up. No response.

Recovered on the couch all day Sunday. No response.

Went to work on Monday. No response.

Monday night, I was sitting at home in my chair that still smelled like the man. I was scrolling through social media and saw The Athlete had, of course, posted something. I sent a text to my friend.

Me: This boy posting shit but can't respond to nobody after days [straight face emoji]

Her: I spoke with him not too long ago and he said "yeah, she's not my speed." He mentioned you had hit him up a few times but he figured you'd get it when he didn't reply back. I told him I'd pass it along since you didn't know what was up.

'Not my speed'. 'Not my speed'??? What in the actual fuck was that supposed to mean?

Conversation. Good.

Sex. Great.

NOT. MY. SPEED.

I really needed someone to explain that one to me. That man barely even knew me. Didn't know a single in-depth thing about me but had already determined I was not his speed. Okay. Hands up. Fine. He didn't like something about me. He didn't think we meshed. Cool. I can get over that. What really pissed me off about this whole thing was the fact that he acted like a child. This 'sweet' and 'nice' 'man' could pick up his phone to post pictures of his shoes every day, but he couldn't type the words "I'm not interested." I gave him the opening. After days of being ignored and treated like last week's trash, I opened it up so he could easily say "I'm not interested."

I wanted to text him a paragraph. Cuss him out. Teach him how you are supposed to treat someone. Tell him to grow the fuck up. Explain to him how he'd made me feel. Typically, I would have done all of those things. I would have sent that paragraph and I would have cried and asked no one in particular why was it so hard for me? Why was I always the one to get ghosted and treated this way? What was I doing wrong? Woe is me.

For some reason, I decided against it—decided I wasn't going to do that. Tears didn't roll over my cheeks. The questions raced through my mind quicker than I could contemplate them. Then I got angry. I decided to sleep on it.

When I woke up the next morning, I was no longer sad or angry and I didn't want to send any long, drawn out message to The Athlete. Even though he didn't feel I deserved to know he had received any of my messages, I felt he had the right to know that I had received his. After thinking about it before I closed my eyes the night before and still feeling the same way when I opened them the next morning, I knew exactly what I was going to say to him.

"Fuck you."

I pressed send with a smile on my face. I hopped in the shower and got ready for my day.

I wasn't expecting a response. I didn't want one, and I wasn't going to spend my day looking for one. That simple 'fuck you' encompassed all he deserved. It wasn't just for him. It was for all of the assholes that have treated me like crap. Yes, I should have known better in some situations. Yes, I may have 'acted crazy' other times. However, that does not give anyone the right to treat people like they are not human. Everyone is a person with feelings and emotions.

So, fuck you.

Fuck you for making me smile just so you could get in my pants.

Fuck you for getting in my bed knowing you're just going to leave in the morning and not look back.

Fuck you for playing mind games for days on end.

Fuck you for ignoring me when I knew you got my message.

Fuck you for making me feel like I'm not worthy of being treated better.

Fuck you.

Fuck you very much.

* * *

A LITTLE WHILE after this happened, I attended a basketball game with the same two girlfriends. Kacy brought her little boy. The other friend was Leo; she was the one who had helped set up the initial conversation between Athlete and me.

Athlete and she were good friends. They considered each other family and I wasn't about to let a little thing like my dislike for the man come between a good friendship—mine and hers or hers with him. I just wouldn't talk about it or bring him up and we'd be good.

Of course, they brought it up. But, it wasn't me, so it doesn't count, right? We all joked about him and the whole situation throughout the game. It was fun times. When the game was over, Leo and I went to my house to chill for a little bit while we decided where we wanted to go get some food.

Kacy called while we were on our way back to my house and said she had lost her wallet. Leo's mom worked at the building where the game had been held, so she called her to see if she could start looking for Kacy's things in the area where we had been sitting. It was a whole thing, but eventually Kacy got her stuff back.

Leo and I drove separately, and when I pulled up to the restaurant, she came over to my car with Kacy on speaker phone.

"Girl!" Kacy hollered out.

"Yeah?" I laughed back.

"Man . . . you won't believe who me and Aiden ran into when we went back to get my wallet." She started laughing.

I looked up at Leo as she held the phone. She had a huge grin on her face.

"Athlete?"

We all started laughing.

"Yup. I asked Aiden if he wanted to take a picture with him and guess what?"

I was already grinning from ear to ear. "What?"

"He said, 'No, Mama. I don't want to,' and Athlete said, 'You don't like me, little man?' and Aiden said, 'No. I don't like basketball.'" She started cracking up and Leo and I joined in.

I was dying laughing. "Man, Aiden should have said, 'No. You're not my speed.'"

SEASON FINALE

Dear Journal,
I'm on my floor again. Drinking wine. I'm okay, though. No tears this time. You know what, Journal? Fork it. I'm just gonna date myself.

I'm not boring or too sweet. I'd rather go up and down on a roller coaster alone. I can't possibly be my own third wheel. I would never not pay myself back that twenty-five dollars. By myself, I can watch porn and fall asleep in the same bed. I would never ghost me, Journal. And if I did, I think that means my life is literally over and I'm pretty positive I can't really transform from a ghost into a zombie.

If I overdose on bacon all by my lonesome, I'll feel safe. I have my own apartment now, so I can't obsess over someone else's. It's okay for me to cling to me. Getting drunk alone can be fun as long as I don't pee on myself. I can be my own superhero. I'm an awesome friend. I'll order my own fresh pizza. If I don't want to share my feelings with anyone but myself and drink some liquor, that's cool.

And, Journal? I'm always going to be my speed.

Here's to Episode 18.
Forever and always,

Cole

ACKNOWLEDGMENTS

Where to begin . . . I honestly don't know. It's been over two years since I've released anything. I've struggled with a lot. With writer's block. With depression. With adulting. It all hit me really, really hard the past couple of years and on some days, I wasn't sure I was going to be able to climb my way out this time. I felt lost and lonely and at the same time, I was pushing a lot of people away. I hid what I was feeling on the inside with laughter and jokes on the outside. I busied myself with the day job and other things. I tried to write, but the words wouldn't come out and then that just made things worse.

And then, one day, I got angry. I got really pissed off and it was then the words started flowing. I wrote down absolutely everything in pieces and chunks and then I read it. It was funny and relatable and I just knew I had to turn this shit into a book. Once I finally got the words out, I started to feel better. I started to feel like there was light cracking through the darkness again.

So, WRITING, you get the first thanks. You saved me.

MY FAMILY, you've always been there for me and accept me for who I am. You put up with my shit all the time and I'm glad we're forced to be a part of each other's lives. I'd still choose you even if we weren't. That being said, I really hope you didn't read this book. You shouldn't know about all of my shenanigans.

JESS AND MAREN, you reached out to me when I went missing there for a little bit and tried to pull me out. I always knew you were there. You waited for me to drag my ass out of my hole and when I did, you opened your arms. Jess, I seriously couldn't do this thing without you.

ALANA, if it wasn't for your help, I probably would have never started a blog and discovered I could still do words. Letting me guest post on yours, showed me my dating life was entertaining to others and I should keep writing that shit down. You'll always be my Biff, whether you want to be or not. We've got a podcast together, so . . . .

TARRAH, I am so excited to be a part of the Girl Power world you created and to be one of your Lurvers. I hope we continue to grow our friendship in this new decade! Your excitement for this book has made me grin ear to ear on all the days.

BLOGGERS, thank you, thank you, thank you. You do so much and I will forever be grateful to you and what you do. We, as authors, couldn't get by without you. I hope you know how much you mean to us.

READERS, I hope you enjoyed that ride! It was kinda fun, right? They (I still don't know who they are) say everything happens for a reason. After putting this book together for you, I know all I've experienced had a purpose. I hope you enjoyed my words and I can't wait to bring you more!

Oh! Hey! It's Cole. I'm just gonna jump in here really quick.

Thank you, T. I'm sure you'll never read this, but I've got to thank you anyway.
If it wasn't for you, I would have never finished writing this book.
Byeeeeeee.

ABOUT THE AUTHOR

S. Cole, otherwise known as Shay, is kind of a hot mess. A fun hot mess, but a mess nonetheless. She gets shit done, but . . . ya get the point. Shay is a daughter, sister, friend, and great worker! She's really awesome at all of those things, but she probably writes best. She has written stories for as long as she can remember. Like, at least since she was seven years old. That's when she wrote her first book. Shay loved conjuring up stories so much, she continued writing them into her twenties. But now, she can drink while she's doing it, so it's even better! Maybe that's why the characters that reside in her little black heart finally bothered her enough that she had to actually *share* them with readers. #wine-mademedoit

Shay grew up in a home where she was taught to embrace her inner nerd and creativity . . . and her short stature. At 5'1, Shay is that short girl who writes about the deranged and devious. For some reason, she strayed from her usual love of crime fiction to write something funny. She once told her friend 'I write dark shit, but when I'm in a dark place, I've got to write light'.

You can stalk S. Cole by following her on Instagram @shay_all_day_ and on Facebook at www.facebook.com/authorscole or visiting her website & blog, www.shayall-day.com

You can follow her on Twitter @shay_all_day_ but you won't get much stalking done there because, even after 3 years, she still sucks at Twitter.

You can contact S. Cole through her email authorscole@gmail.com

Made in the USA
Columbia, SC
20 February 2020

87942785R00120